BEFORE THERE IS NOWHERE TO STAND
Palestine | Israel: Poets Respond to the Struggle

BEFORE THERE IS
NOWHERE TO STAND

Palestine | Israel:
Poets Respond to the Struggle

edited by
Joan Dobbie & Grace Beeler
with Edward Morin

LOST HORSE PRESS
Sandpoint, Idaho

ACKNOWLEDGMENTS

The editors thank the anthology poets and others who contributed much time and energy: Elaine Weiss, Ingrid Wendt, Naomi Shihab Nye, Alicia Ostriker, Ellen Rifkin, Mary Anne Grady Flores, Vivien Sansour, Samuel Hazo, Khaled Mattawa, Reja-e Busailah, Ibrahim Muhawi, Deborah Noble, David Solomon Thaler, Michael James, Emily Fox, Ellen Thaler Beeler, Gustavo and Tiago Furtado.

Grateful thanks to financial contributors, some of whom are listed below, and others who remain anonymous:

Frances Payne Adler, Drs. Monisha and Salman Akhtar, Wendy Barker, Ellen Thaler Beeler, Daniel Bellm, M. Jan Bender, Arlene Chasek, Helen Frost, Charles Gross and Joyce Smith, Charlotte Gross, Quinton Hallett, Thomas Hertz and Sarah Browning, Suzanne Hyman, George and Cynthia Kokis, Melissa Lane, Irwin and Charlotte Mandel, Joan and James Murray, Deborah Noble, Sylvia Pafenyk, Peter Pitzele, Annie H. Popkin, Jane D. Schaburg, Ronnie Scharfman, Harold and Vivien Shapiro, Ronald A. Sharp, Ernest Von Simson, David Stone, Cy and Lois Swartz, David Solomon Thaler, and Joyce and Ed Turner.

A portion of the proceeds from each book sold will be donated to *Oasis of Peace/ Neve Shalom/ Wahat al-Salam,* a village jointly established by Jewish and Palestinian Arab citizens of Israel that is engaged in educational work for peace, equality and understanding between the two peoples. For more information on *Wahat al-Salam/Neve Shalom,* please visit their web site at *www.nswas.org.*

Cover art by David Luckert, *Vestibule*, oil on canvas, 43" x 36"
Book design by Christine Holbert
Lost Horse Press Senior Editor: Christi Kramer

FIRST EDITION

This and other fine titles by Lost Horse Press — including our award-winning Human Rights Series — may be found online at www.losthorsepress.org.

Library of Congress Cataloging-in-Publication Data

Before there is nowhere to stand : Palestine/Israel : poets respond to the struggle / [editors, Joan Dobbie and Grace Beeler].
      p. cm.
ISBN 978-0-9839975-8-0 (alk. paper)
1. Arab-Israeli conflict—Poetry. 2. Jerusalem—Poetry. I. Dobbie, Joan, 1946- II. Beeler, Grace.
PN6110.A76B44 2012
808.810095694'42—dc23
                                    2012014896

TABLE OF CONTENTS

|||

IV

V

DEDICATION

We dedicate this effort to two young Palestinians — Khaldoun Sammoudi and Ahmad Maslman — who were killed within a week of each other at the same Israeli checkpoint in January 2011, and equally to Rabbi Myron Kinberg (February 1945 - April 1996), whose love for Israel did not stop him from being a tireless and dedicated proponent of justice, peace and equality in that land.

INTRODUCTION BY ALICIA OSTRIKER

A major holiday in Israel, *Yom Ha'atzma'ut*, Independence Day, is celebrated with marches, flags, speeches, an air show, fireworks, picnics and barbecues. It commemorates the end of the British Mandate of Palestine and the founding of the state of Israel on May 14, 1948. It is the equivalent of our July 4th.

In Arabic the equivalent term is *Yam Al Nakba*, Catastrophe Day. For Palestinians, May 15th marks the expulsion and flight of upwards of eight hundred thousand Palestinians from their towns and villages in the face of Israeli troop advances and violence, the massacres that took place at that time, and the reduction of hundreds of thousands to the status of refugees. The day is marked by rallies and protests against what Jews call "the situation" and what Palestinians call "the occupation."

Joy and pain, triumph and humiliation, fear and zealotry, rage and martyrdom. Since 1948, through six or seven more wars and one failed peace process after another, through expanded Jewish settlements and Muslim suicide bombings, through brutal assassinations, murder, torture, kidnapping, the threat of annihilation and the reality of homes destroyed, through the passionate certitude of ultra-religious Jews and ultra-religious Muslims that the land belongs to them exclusively and that the Other should disappear, the precious fragment of land known as Israel, known as Palestine, has been holy to too many people. Is there, can there be, an end to this conflict? This ping-pong of violence and retaliation? This wound that refuses to heal?

In a visit to Israel with the "pro-Israel-pro-peace" organization *J Street* in the spring of 2010, I hear over and over that "everyone" knows what the outlines of a two-state agreement will be, yet the politicians are unable to reach it. In Hebron we meet with activists in the growing Palestinian non-violence movement, with Aziz who says "If I choose revenge on those who killed my brother, I choose their path," with Ali who recalls when he came out of prison, his mother had invited Israeli families to their home and "for the first time I saw Jews cry." A sweet young woman soldier at a Gaza checkpoint confides in us, "I have to wear a gun at all times. I take it off when I take a shower, and I think: what if an alarm goes off and I have to run naked for a shelter? I'd rather die." A peacenik from the Sderot kibbutz—where rockets from Gaza have rained down night after night—describes his network of secret communication with ordinary Gazans who, if their names were known, might be shot. In Jerusalem we join 300 Jewish and Arab student types in the weekly Friday demonstration against evicting Arab families in Sheikh Jarrah, a neighborhood of East Jerusalem. The lively drumming and call-and-response chants led by a kid in dreadlocks is all filmed by a plainclothesman with a video camera, and IDF soldiers hustle the crowd into one area, but nobody seems perturbed. Arrests of peaceful demonstrators have occurred on other Fridays, but not this time. Perhaps the hope for peace is not dead after all?

The need to go on hoping forms the bedrock of this book. True, there are poems here that dwell on agonized memories of the holocaust and the shock of realizing that descendants of survivors are themselves "shelling the houses of the innocent," killing children, killing grandmothers. Some focus on the horrors of suicide bombing, and the irony that limbs of bombers and victims inextricably mingle. In a poetic sequence called "The Situation," Joy Ladin portrays the anomie and spatial disorientation her Tel Aviv students experience during an Intifada. Her poem "The Situation: An Exclusive Simulcast" evokes the Biblical twins Jacob and Esau, and the yearning "For the twin/Who craves what you crave /Who lived where you live/ To admit/ He never existed." Tom Berman evokes the impartial feeding habits of "the Hate" in mosques and markets, yeshiva study halls and emergency wards where it feeds fat; "All manner of worshippers/ pay homage."

A number of these poems document specific historical events. The furious run-on momentum of Sandy Polishuk's prose-poem "Possession" recounts the founding of the Jewish settlement in Hebron, with the rabbi's wife Miriam Levinger as triumphal Zionist zealot:

and now there are four hundred Jews living in the Arab's city and even with three soldiers for every settler can the government protect them because even though Miriam was victorious and lives in the city she wasn't able to stop the peace process but she will stay calling on ancient history and saying that the Bible is their deed since this land was promised to them and everyone knows that but what of the others who are there who will stay there too no matter how badly they are treated because they too believe it belongs to them and so it is . . .

Yasmin Snounu gives witness to the use of white phosphorus against civilians in Gaza during Israel's Operation Cast Lead. Carolyne Wright describes, in excruciating slow motion, the death of Rachel Corrie, run over by a bulldozer while she demonstrated against bulldozing Arab homes. Ellen Bass and Vivien Sansour each wrestle with the incident of two brothers shot in Gaza by an Israeli soldier who refuses to let their father take the still-living one through a checkpoint to a hospital; Sansour's bitter journalistic title is "Live from Gaza."

Is there a single place to lay blame? Not really. Doreen Stock imagines a dead Palestinian girl wrapped in "the very bolt of silk the arms/ were wrapped in, the Chinese Russian American Israeli/British Iranian arms . . ." Judy Kronenfeld's poem "Clean," triggered by seeing a van labeled *Crime Scene Cleaners, Inc.*, ends by demanding that "the war presidents and prime/ministers and militia leaders/ for whom war is holy . . . be each given one small toothbrush,/ and the sentence: scour this blood."

The absurdity of the situation is highlighted in David Gersahator's "Dividing Jerusalem: "You take the olives/ I'll take the figs/you take the sparrows / I'll take the doves . . ." The pathos of exile is highlighted in Naomi Shihab Nye's suite of poems honoring her exiled and dying father asking "Does the land remember me?" or Yousef al Qedra lamenting being "stretched like a string that doesn't belong to an instrument." The double urgency of loss, of need, is highlighted in Johnmichael Simon's series of poignant metaphors:

> They moved out of Gaza . . .
> feeling like ivy ripped off the walls
> like irrigation pipes torn from the soil . . .
> They moved into Gaza . . .
> Feeling like water released from a dam . . .

Yet hope, too, surges toward release. What feeds that spring is irresistible human empathy. Rachel Barenblat remembers that Isaac and Ishmael are both sons of the Biblical patriarch Abraham, and imagines "Abraham's dark eyes in every face" at his burial. Rochelle Mass looks from a kitchen window on Mount Gilboa and wonders whether a housewife in Jenin is processing olives like her, and "if that woman/ is looking my way—/I would ask if she's angry/if she's afraid." Moments of tenderness or humor across the boundaries of supposed enmity illuminate poems by Dana Negev, Carol Alena Aronoff, Susan Martin and Hadassah Haskale, among others. Monica Raymond's exuberant sestina "In Cana," remembering that the town's Arabic name is Qana, that Jesus performed his first miracle at a wedding there—turning water into wine—and only later said he brought not peace but a sword, scolds today's "apocalyptic idiots, Muslim, Christian, and Jew," and offers her "disarmament proposal":

> *What if we acted as if the whole world were a wedding*
> *with good wine till the end? What if you left your sword*
> *at the door and never retrieved it?*

"Nation shall not lift up sword against nation," prophesied Isaiah in the 8th century BCE, "neither shall they learn war any more." Presently we are not holding our breath waiting for that moment. Jews have a story. Arabs have a story. Jews and

Arabs can both be experts at seeing themselves as victims and the other side as implacable foes. As my engineer friend in Tel Aviv says, "It all started when he hit me back." The story of Israel/Palestine is ugly, tragic, human. But the book you hold in your hands exists to remind you that the story is not finished. The long, lyric, haunting poem, composed by Peter Marcus, consists of alternating passages by Mahmoud Darwish and Yehuda Amichai, the recently deceased most beloved poets of Palestine and Israel respectively. Here are the closing lines of this "Dialog Beneath the Light":

> *I touch your mouth that now, perhaps,*
> *will sing.*

> You will carry me and I will carry you.
> Strangers are also brothers.

> *When a man's far away from his country for a long time*
> *his language becomes more precise, more pure.*

> Share my bread, drink my wine,
> Don't leave me alone like a tired willow.

A NOTE BY CHRISTI KRAMER

There is, perhaps, an imagination that can transform the violent world we live in. Poetry holds this possibility. If language itself may efface or serve to reproduce narratives that diminish or that normalize oppression, where is the difference? Might poetry open to a telling that is full; might it be a place of witness, for meeting of self and other? In it, may a lone reader find (what you may call) courage or solidarity, humanity; or recognize in the creative act proof of resilience?

Or, shall we share Mahmoud Darwish's stance, that "Every beautiful poem is an act of resistance."

You may find the poems gathered here to be invitation. Or you might understand this anthology as a response to a call for poetic imagination.

In 2009, the editors, Joan Dobbie and Grace Beeler, both descendants of Holocaust survivors, reacting to Israel's Operation Cast Lead, the Gaza massacre, issued a call for poetry. The ad, first posted in *Poets & Writers* read, *"Are you Jewish or Palestinian? Of Palestinian or Jewish heritage? Please submit poetry for an anthology that strives for understanding in these troubled times. All points of view wanted in the belief that poetry can create understanding and understanding can dull hatred."* In response, the process that then followed embodied much of the complex dynamic of the conflict itself. Editors, while not wanting to foreclose any possible reading, were met with the need to attend to disparity of voice, asymmetry, and incongruence of historical awareness. To come close to approaching the goals they had set forth and to which contributing poets responded, and to help scaffold the anthology, the editors solicited an introduction from Palestinian poets. The anthology may fall short here: This didn't happen.

Vivien Sansour gave permission to print her correspondence in lieu of an introduction, along with two of her poems. Even as the editors do not assume there to be a singular Palestinian or Jewish "voice," Vivien's letter may echo opposition and challenge normalization. Because what is absent is as telling as what is present.

—*Christi Kramer*
March 2012

IN LIEU OF AN INTRODUCTION BY VIVIEN SANSOUR

5 January 2011

Dear Joan and Grace,

Please accept my sincerest apologies for being so late in responding to you. I have been reading the manuscript and really struggling with it to be honest. For the sake of full integrity I would like to share with you a couple of things. I do not feel a just representation and I am afraid that in the context of an unfortunately misunderstood political reality the anthology, although I know and trust that it is well intentioned, perpetuates an idea that I am very uncomfortable with and that is of framing the situation as two people who just need to get along and who just don't understand each other. I have been discussing it with my dear friend Ayelet who is a former Israeli soldier and currently lives in Los Angeles as she refuses to return to Israel and have her kids serve in the army. We had both performed poems we wrote to each other in the past and we have found that, unfortunately, the reality of a military occupation becomes clouded when the message of "bridging gaps of understanding between two people who just don't get along" is perpetuated. In that spirit, I write you with my deepest regrets because I feel I cannot participate in your anthology; not in an introduction nor with my poems.

As I was making my trip from Jenin to the U.S. (via Jordan because I, like most Palestinians, am not allowed to use the airport in Tel Aviv) our car was stopped on the road by an Israeli checkpoint and we were forced out of the car and made to stand in the cold for half an hour. After being humiliated and screamed at by a young Israeli soldier *(move, stop, walk, go back)* we were finally let through to make it to the bridge to cross with thirteen different checks and stops in Palestinian-only buses that we were stuffed into like animals. It is hard for me on a personal level as well to compare and equate my experiences in the same context as my oppressor. The poem

vii

for the people of Sderot, for example, makes it look like we all suffer from the same demon of fear. While all human suffering is awful, in the grander political context there is a political force, a powerful military force that the people of Sderot are supported and protected by. They are part of a system that is systemically and slowly exterminating an indigenous population. Not to mention that Sderot is a settlement built on stolen land. The people of Gaza are imprisoned with no access to sea or land to run away to even. I do not want to focus on these details, I just want to explain why in the struggle to achieve justice, which is the only way to peace, I am growing more and more convinced alongside my Israeli and international colleagues who are also struggling for justice, that it is important for us to present the situation as it is: A military occupation and not a conflict between two people. Jews, Muslims, Christians have lived together in Palestine before 1948 and it was not until a European colonial project was started in the beginning of the 1900s that we started "not to get along."

Unfortunately, I do not see myself participating in such a context. Perhaps I would if one day justice is served and we are in a state of reconciliation. However, this reconciliation whether through poetry or otherwise is not possible at this point. As I would like to describe it, it is like having to sit down with my rapist and understand his pain while he is still penetrating me.

My only regret is that I have taken a long time to come to this conclusion and I am afraid I have caused you an inconvenience in your process. But I would have also done you injustice to write an introduction that would not be in integrity with where I stand nor with how I think the struggle for justice is best served.

Respectfully,
Vivien Sansour

. . . I am also sad to inform you that at that same checkpoint where I stood before the new year, a 25-year-old man from a village close by here where I often work, named Khaldoun Sammoudi was shot because he misunderstood soldiers' command to stop. He was shot several times and died at the checkpoint. Another one, 21-year-old Ahmad Maslman, was shot a week after. I crossed two weeks before he was killed. It could have been me if I had not understood and obeyed the commands. If we could honor their spirits by mentioning their names. I think of this young man and I wonder perhaps he was a writer or a poet or a talented farmer. We will never know what hidden talents died before he got to tap into them.

Vivien Sansour

We are not anti-Israel or anti-Palestine. We are pro-human being and pro-peace. Our hope has been and still is that we have created a space where all people involved in this conflict are recognized and respected. Like many of our readers, we are appalled by all war. Violence, especially when directed toward innocents, is never acceptable. Only when we can actually listen to one another and acknowledge each other as human beings can there begin to be work toward peace. This is our hope with this book, which was not conceived as an avenue to vilify, but as a means of understanding, and conceivably, of creating tolerance. It has to do with faith in the power of poetry to reveal truth, and of truth to do good.

When we put out the call for poetry, we had no idea what sort of response we would get: we were overwhelmed by the quality of poetry that was submitted. We sent out the manuscript, hoping that an established press would take on our project. Lost Horse Press agreed to publish the anthology, but upon reviewing our manuscript, found it to be an unfinished work, too long and too out of balance, with many more poems by Jews than Arabs.

With the help of Lost Horse Press senior editor, Christi Kramer, and of poet and translator, Edward Morin, we set about paring down and bringing balance to the manuscript. The editing process was not easy, and took many months and a lot of compromise, but in the end, a book emerged that, in the words of Lost Horse Press, is "beautiful, balanced and just plain wonderful."

Our wish is that you will take the time to read with an open mind and heart the work that is contained in this book. You may find yourself transported into the minds and worlds of people very like you, and some whose lives and views are quite different. Please take time to contemplate who they are and what their perspectives are. We have felt from the beginning, and continue to feel, that this book may lead toward positive change in how people perceive one another.

Ruth Fogelman

JERUSALEM, CITY OF PRAYER

In the market place, in front of copper scales, round weights,
On a wicker stool,
Sits a white-turbaned man with full white beard.
His white jalabiyah covering arms and legs,
Eyes closed,
Palms over ears,
He sways as he chants Koran verses.

At the Western Wall
Stands a black-hatted man with full white beard.
His black coat covering arms and trousers,
Eyes closed,
One hand holds a book,
The other caresses ancient stones.
He sways as he whispers prayers and psalms.

A five-minute walk separates them,
A thick, invisible wall separates them —

The Sons of Abraham.

Samuel Hazo

FOR FAWZI IN JERUSALEM

Leaving a world too old to name
and too undying to forsake,
I flew the cold, expensive sea
toward Columbus' mistake
where life could never be the same

for me. In Jerash on the sand
I saw the colonnades of Rome
bleach in the sun like skeletons.
Behind a convalescent home,
armed soldiers guarded no man's land

between Jordanians and Jews.
Opposing sentries frowned and spat.
Fawzi, you mocked in Arabic
this justice from Jehoshophat
before you shined my Pittsburgh shoes

for nothing. Why you never kept
the coins I offered you is still
your secret and your victory.
Saying you saw marauders kill
your father while Beershebans wept

for mercy in their holy war,
you told me how you stole to stay
alive. You must have thought I thought
your history would make me pay
a couple of piastres more

than any shine was worth—and I
was ready to—when you said, "No,

I never take. I never want
America to think I throw
myself on you. I never lie."

I watched your young but old man's stare
demand the sword to flash again
in blood and flame from Jericho
and leave the bones of these new men
of Judah bleaching in the air

like Roman stones upon the plain
of Jerash. Then you faced away.
Jerusalem, Jerusalem,
I asked myself if I could pray
for peace and not recall the pain

you spoke. But what could praying do?
Today I live your loss in no
man's land but mine, and every time
I talk of fates not just but so,
Fawzi, my friend, I think of you.

Rick Black

BOUGAINVILLEA

Candles are not yet
        aglow like sapphires,
                the braided *challah* is still uncut,
                        quiet beckons,
and the last #18 bus
        is packed.
                People are returning from Mahane Yehuda,
the outdoor market of Jerusalem —
inhale the scents of cinnamon, cardamom and curry,
piled high in mounds,
the barrels of pickles, sour and half sour,
the pickled herring, creamed herring, matjes herring
and piles of fresh dates, smooth and sweet,
and chocolate *ruggelach* and *babke*, oval sesame rolls,
challahs with raisins, and hot pita,

and crowds shoving, bustling, hustling, bargaining,
        shouting, mobbing,
elbowing each other, shuffling along beneath the bare
        electric bulbs
hanging,
suspended like the lights of the George Washington Bridge
above the *ducans,*
"*Melafifon* — 40 shekels."
"*Tut, tutim* — fresh strawberries. *Pilpale* — peppers."

Dressed in *streimels,* flowing robes, silk skirts, pushing
baby carriages, shlepping plastic shopping bags,
speaking a mélange of tongues — Hebrew, Arabic, French,
        English and German —
shoppers ebb and flow like waves rushing and receding
from shore,

from one merchant to another. They gather like flocks
of seagulls, then disperse past the green-leaved clumps
of garlic, bulbous clumps, dry, hard like the noses of passersby,
bright, shiny eggplants, globular. Go ahead,
imbibe the scent of fresh cut oranges, tongue the bits of halvah,
gently press the avocado skins and squeeze the tomatoes
at dusk on Shabbat,
and taste the loaves of challah woven into the prayer shawl
of our people's history.

Emitting plumes of black diesel smoke,
the bus leaves the market, stops at the Central Bus Station
and chugs up Mt. Herzl into the ethereal, blood-soaked air
of Jerusalem
and there —
in the fading, tarnished light descending
on the city and the Jerusalem pines —
just past Yad Vashem —
there,
the bus, its red and white sides gleaming,
clinging to the hill stubbornly
and climbing up it like bougainvillea,
there
the bus explodes:
skewering flesh, shattering glass, shrieking in the quiescent
     streets,
and sobbing,
there
overturned like a beetle,
helpless, writhing, unsilent

there
like a crushed violin,
its mangled strings
twisted
          notes
shrieking in the sky

                    and the ambulances wail
"Holy, holy, holy!"

and the pines
in the golden, Sabbath sunlight,
          (for candles will soon be lit),

glow ineffably, more beautiful
than ever,

and God remains
in his own way, silent.

We are near *Ein Kerem*,
Ein keloheinu, ein, ein, ein . . .
"There is no
          God
      like our God.

There is no
          king
      like our king.
There is no
          redeemer
      like our redeemer."

And the angels cry
and the ambulances wail
and survivors lie on the pavement, wounded,
having fallen back down
in the Vitebesk street,

    a violin's strings
  broken. But, if you listen
carefully,
          perhaps you'll hear wind

in the pines,
perhaps you'll see
            starlight glisten
off shattered glass,

                      and off bougainvillea petals
that are still climbing,
reaching up

in prayer.

Nizar Qabbani

JERUSALEM

Jerusalem, luminous city of prophets,
shortest path between heaven and earth!

Jerusalem, you of the myriad minarets,
become a beautiful little girl with burned fingers.
City of the Virgin, your eyes are sad.
Shady oasis where the Prophet passed,
the stones of your streets grow sad,
the towers of mosques downcast.
City swathed in black, who'll ring the bells
at the Holy Sepulchre on Sunday mornings?
Who will carry toys to children
on Christmas Eve?
City of sorrows, a huge tear
trembling on your eyelid,
who'll save the Bible?
Who'll save the Qur'an?
Who will save Christ, who will save man?

Jerusalem, beloved city of mine,
tomorrow your lemon trees will bloom,
your green stalks and branches rise up joyful,
and your eyes will laugh. Migrant pigeons
will return to your holy roofs
and children will go back to playing.
Parents and children will meet
on your shining streets,
my city, city of olives and peace.

Translated by Sharif Elmusa and Naomi Shihab Nye

David Miller

MEMORIES OF THE WAILING WALL

1.

an Israeli soldier
my age
patrolling the top of the wall
nothing above him but sky
below him all of Jerusalem.

he had rifle slung over his shoulder,
a *Galil*.

I recognized it
because my father raised me
shooting guns.

It was our religion.

2.

a curtain separated
the men from the women

pieces of paper
scraps of prayer

folded like bird wings
into the stones.
I approached the wall
tucked in a prayer.

even though I could read Hebrew letters
I didn't know what they meant.

my own prayer
was to get laid.

3.
In the crowd were girl soldiers. They looked the same
age as me, had the same flares of acne. They laughed and
shared cigarettes over their Uzis.

4.
an elderly Hassid asked me if I spoke French.
"un petit peu," I said.
He held my shoulder
and started saying Kaddish.

Not knowing what to do, I started saying it with him,
matching his smoky voice
then trailing away
when it got to the parts I couldn't remember.

5.
Somewhere behind
the Frenchman and I:
my dad
who hadn't fought in a war
but always studied them

our tour guide Yakov
who'd fought in all 5 Israeli wars
but didn't talk about them

my grandfather
who shipped out to the Pacific
just before the war ended

my grandmother
who waited for him
collecting letters

my brother
who'd grown up with me
watching wars on television.

6.
As we said Kaddish I felt everything fall away.

7.
Was it God I felt?
or lonesomeness / confusion?

Was it seeing kids disguised as soldiers
armed to fight kids disguised as terrorists?

or was it being a kid disguised as a tourist?

8.
Was it looking at
the house-sized blocks of stone,

and imagining them carried on broken backs?

Was it all the stories
I'd learned in Sunday School?

Abraham going to sacrifice Isaac?

Was all of it
connecting to me

now that I was here?

9.
All I knew was that the truck drivers, the carpenters, the soldiers,
the laundrymen, the beggars, the newspaper vendors, the garbage
collectors: everyone was Jewish.

10.
Which felt good in some way, perhaps the way Yakov
    kept reminding me:
I could always come here to live. It was the Jewish homeland.

But in another way I felt like I always did:
like I'd get a better view from atop the desert mountains
away from the crowds
and the shadow of the wall.

Seema V. Atalla

GIFT

One afternoon
you tried to give me Jerusalem

Knobby onion domes
purple windows stained with God's tears
carrot juice, cobblestones
your girlhood ringlets, sunny laugh
the very gates of the Old City
so faithfully embroidered

It was impossible—too precious
the gift, too short the time
or so I thought then

You suffered, like Jerusalem
and left us

Now I think of your finger
the one that clutched a live wire
the day you nearly fell off the roof
the pinkie forever clenched, scarred
stunted
a lifeline that never healed.

Decades later, oceans away, I want to tell you:
I have it.
The gift you tried to give me, I've found it
it's been with me all along

Jerusalem like a blue bead embedded in my tongue
Jerusalem like a rock in the pit of my stomach
ring whose metal digs into my skin
ache under one rib, which never goes away

Jerusalem
the pain cross-stitched into my heart
with a needle that pierces both ways:
going in, and coming out.

Alicia Ostriker

WHAT IS NEEDED AFTER FOOD

The darkness doesn't war against the light,
It carries us forward
to another light. . . .

In my land, called holy,
they won't let eternity be:
they've divided it into little religions,
zoned it for God-zones,
broken it into fragments of history,
sharp and wounding unto death.

—Yehuda Amichai

—for Linda Zisquit

And so beautiful it cracks the bones, especially Jerusalem
with the lustre of her stones, the hurt in her eyes,
and our dreams for her children: a triangle,

beauty, despair, hope . . . the whole *mishpochah*
pulling three ways at the same time
like the people in so many families,

fighting but joined at the hip, or call it a sandwich,
despair the filling embraced by the bread of beauty and hope,
like a manna we eat every day, sent from above,

while on earth in Jerusalem my friend's husband and son
relax from a sabbath meal, like well-fed beasts,
happily slumped watching the aftermath

of a game where the Nazareth team has just won
and vaulted from the bottom of their league
to the top, the players have stripped off their shirts,

hugging and dancing, circle dancing, belly dancing,
waving at crowds in the stands to make them cheer louder.
The coach strips his shirt from his hairy barrel chest,

climbs a wire fence, wobbles and waves his hips.
When someone asks how he feels about his team
(a mix of Jews, Moslems, and one Nigerian,

he himself is Druze), he punches the air
and roars, *I beat them all! I beat Arafat! I beat Sharon!*
I show them we love each other! We watch a while,

the celebration is still going on when we quit
to go back to the kitchen, where loaves of beauty and hope
stand on the counter and the cup of despair goes on the shelf,

my friend and I, we don't ask for much, we read Amichai,
we're not messianic, we don't expect utopia, which is anyway
another name for a smiling prison,

but love is a good idea, we think, why on earth not.
Simple women that we are, simple mothers cleaning up
the kitchen after one meal to make it ready for the next.

Diab Rabie

SWEARING BY YOUR JERUSALEM

The nightingale stopped singing and mourned the lost land;
It wandered into spaces where winds held command.
Tired by many nights of flight, it took its rest,
But not at wondrous sites or near a female breast.
It once rejoiced in singing, now it merely cries
All night till morning, and it will not shut its eyes.
Memories with bleeding wounds cried out in disgust:
How could you leave the country and abandon your trust.
Your trees shade strangers who oppress and occupy.
Rise, throw off the veil of shame none can justify.
Can the oppressed despise sharp swords and keep their pride?
Face daily insults silently and step aside?
You will regain your land only by sword and spear;
With their help, people will see justice reappear.
Youth came into this world to battle with their hands;
Brook no pollution in this holiest of lands.
I swear by "Your Jerusalem," maimed Palestine,
That Arab flags will wave above you for all time.

Translated by George Khoury and Edward Morin

This poem was published in the Arabic language newspaper, *Sameer,* in
New York City one month after the UN resolution in 1947 to divide Palestine.

Sabena Stark

HIGH HOLY DAYS

Jerusalem, October 4th, 2000

Lost in the dry heart of Yerushalayim
God, like a broken messenger
Sleeping through the long day's heat
Ears ringing with the sobs of children,
Lies hidden under the shade of a fig tree.
Could these be the Holy Days
The Holy One intended us to sanctify
In this parched corner of the world?

Buses still run on my street
People in the neighborhood mourn their lost soldiers
I am quiet in the white cage of my little porch
With my newspapers and cold tea
Only photographs
And a camera's moving pictures
Show how blood is spilling
Across the blistering earth of Palestine
Of Yisrael

A shofar wails again and again from an apartment across the road
My ears ache with weariness
I hear the Holy Days unfolding
To the sound of gunfire crackling
Toward the young bodies of Umm el-Fahm
And Nablus
Wives and mothers are crying
Shrieking with rage
Beaten and cursing for the lives of their boys
Whose flesh was torn and shattered by rubber bullets

Last night Avinu Malkeinu lifted from the throats
Of the observant
While well-armed soldiers aimed their guns
At a terrified child near Netzarim
Instead of at the snipers behind him
Armies of children threw their bodies
Their stones, their souls
At machine guns
At missiles dropping from the sky

Death to the Jews echoed from the west
A fragile, ancient alliance ripped apart
As windows of stores were broken in Jaffa
And on a side road in the north
God is Great rang out
At the point-blank murder of a young father
Bringing his old car to be fixed
The main artery to Akko
And Sfat is closed

I watched young soldiers wearing kippas
Supplicate to the Almighty
In our pretty wood-paneled shul
While bullets seared the bodies
Of their brothers guarding Joseph's Tomb
Our Mother Rachel wept
As her resting place was stoned

Yom Kippur looms ahead
Outrage and desolation
Burns into the streets
Pelted into the eyes of the world
Names of God hurled like fire
Like death
The prayers of Yerushalayim
From all corners of the world
Slip like water through a sieve

Onto the torn hopes of mothers and fathers
Their fingers despaired of their music
Their voices joined lamenting life
Blessing the Eternal

I am quiet on my little porch
Wondering if You are hiding
Under the tree below my balcony
Wondering if You expect me to call out Your Attributes
To fast and wear white
Or to rip and rend my clothes

Aftab Yusuf Shaikh

JERUSALEM

If this city were a woman,
She must have earned a bad name by now,
For the number of swords unsheathed,
For the cauldrons of blood shed,
For the haunting silence that rings in wombs,
For the innocent childhoods weeded,

But, No!
This is a city, and a holy one!
Holy for whom? The ones who heap
unholiness on it.

O children of Abraham!
You are not pagans or witches,
You must remember very sharply,
That the shedding of blood cleanses nothing,
And nothing cleanses the shedding of blood,

Man remembers the Promises of God,
But very casually forgets
The Promise God took from him!

Jerry Newman

THE STONES OF OLD JERUSALEM

Any one of the stones of old Jerusalem
could crush a man or woman
far sturdier than you or me,
a family, an army, a nation,
an idea.

If I forget thee, Oh Jerusalem,
may I also forget the others
who coveted you as I once did, who offered
to trade their blood for mine,
for you.

Jerusalem!
Your cellars are awash in blood!
The blood of your worshippers
have thrice three times made your streets
unclean!

Nothing will remain, in the end, but memories:
the ancient enmities, the Covenant
between man and "God," the rise
of the Christians and their defeat,
the Mohammedans . . .

Each left their markers, their portions
of holy real estate, blood,
in the end, more enduring than stone.

Jerusalem, somewhere between Golgotha
and a spiritual Disneyland,
where is enacted over and over again
the raising of the temple, its destruction,

the rebuilding of it, the second destruction,
the dispersion of its people . . .

In the end there is always the problem
of distinguishing the real
from the real estate.

Adonis (Ali Ahmad Said Esber)

Excerpt: CONCERTO FOR JERUSALEM

1. Heavenly Summation

Up there, up above,
Look at her dangling from the sky's throat.
Look at her being fenced with the eyelashes of angels.

No one can go afoot toward her.
One can use his forehead, palms, perhaps his navel.

Barefoot, knock on her door.
A prophet will open it, and teach you how to walk, and
     how to bow.

A stage play directed by the all-powerful, the almighty.
And the lord does thus for all his sons:

—"Here I am, a silhouette of Jerusalem,"
     cried a three-headed dummy on the stage, then exited.

•

Bait al-Maqdes complained of its ruins to the lord
And the Lord revealed to it:
"I will fill you with faces that long for you
     the way doves long for their young."
—Fear God, O Ka'ab, how can you say this?
     Does Bait al-Maqdes have a tongue?
—Yes, and a heart like you.
          (reported by Ka'ab)

A stage play directed by the all-powerful, the almighty.

For so long I've begged bread to criticize salt.
Many times, I've heard people ask me, whispering,
    "Why is death always late in Jerusalem, while
    the march of life becomes another death?"
And how can a head be imprisoned in the cellar of
    the words that it had invented?

Truly, the unknown becomes deceptive in Jerusalem, and
    he is the master of all deceivers.
In a corner, in the farthest reaches of my desert,
A gazelle weeps.

●

Time rushing through the streets of Jerusalem, I
    know your name.
I was commanded to offer you the juice of uranium.
I will tell the moon to sign your book, and the sun
    to date the signing.
And look, here are walls spilling the milk of their sadness
On your ground, celebrating you.
Time, you know,
That the ants stand higher than all the planets:
Ants spoke to Solomon,
But the planets never could.
Perhaps this is why ants can prophesy:
Belts, masks, trenches, earth movers,
Bombs, missiles, suitcases, tires, and electronic brains:

●

These are the coming days.
Perhaps that is why
The sky has become a secret hole in history's ceiling.

"Jerusalem, land of summoning and judgement."
        (a Hadith narrated by Abu Dhar)
"He who dies in Jerusalem, is like one who dies in the heavens."
        (a Hadith narrated by Abu Huraira)

But, here's Imru' al-Qais!
He is passing by Jerusalem as he heads to Byzantium.
Before his feet touch the threshold, he says:
        To the blood shed on the shores of the Mediterranean
        From the beginnings, a ravaged history.
        To the earth's history
        A heavenly summation named Jerusalem.
        But why are there only two kinds of people in it:
            The dead who live in poverty,
            And the living who live in graves?

                            •

Day and night wrestle, each trying to choke the other
        in the name of Jerusalem.
Time made a documentary film of the battle.
But Imru' al-Qais said, departing,
In the beginning was the word,
In the beginning of the word was blood.

A stage play directed by the all-powerful, almighty.

Imru' al-Qais have you tired of walking these
        streets divided by the unknown?
How excellent they are at kidnapping?
How powerful their walls at intercepting people's words?
Every time you try to embrace a woman, a guard asks you:
Do you have the heavens' permission?
Indeed, all the fruits on these streets are bitter.
Nonetheless, you go on walking, more persistently
Than a hungry male ant,

Making of your steps strings for music that has yet to arrive,
Edged by reeds of erect dreams that the eggs of doubt shun.

                              •

You suspect that your bed is another night altogether
And someone is whispering to you:
Night lies, as usual, even though he is the sun's
     most loyal friend.
You are used to starting from point zero by now
Because you have caught the scent of eternities.
Your grandmother, that Ukhazi sky, used to tuck money into her
     sons' pockets
Which was nothing but dice,
And she demanded they spread them at night on
     the sands of the stars, if they wanted to finish their dreams.
And according to her commands,
They did lay their qasidas on the sand
In blessing and celebration.

You are now under another sky. Bleeding walls surround you.
Heads that are almost cut off speak without ceasing.
Have no fear, dear wind,
Forests on fire hide behind the traps you have set.
And there are springs spilling blood from the eye
     of the needle the sky holds in her hand.

                              •

—The words of swords and spears and they prey
     on anyone who can see.
—Angels have preferred to become lovers where
     the smoke of Arab musk is a space for their banishment
     between Hejaz and Jerusalem.
—Your sky is a linguistic etching. Your earth is
     weighted with delusions. Whenever a word
     heaves among the etchings, the teeth of history rattle,

and heads roll in all directions, while the
stars appear like bundles of straw.
— The history of a milk that escaped the bosoms of
their mothers to feed the moon and the stars.
— When the storm attacks, it has no weapon except
our bodies. It fills our days with black clouds that
no light can read.
— This is how we make coffins before their time is due.
We anoint them with the perfume of pre-
creation. In their names, we slit the artery of the
earth to feed the veins of the unknown.
— History, read your horoscope, and you will see
how delusions are turned into towers of facts.
— The body of history surrenders on astrology's
bed. Here it is unbuttoning its clothes.

•

The wind reads the roses.
Perfumes write them.

A woman in love entered her garden in Jerusalem,
where her lover lives.
The flowers form a net that tangled her steps.
She laughed and said,
Must I then sew a new dress for every flower?
Yesterday when I met her, night whispered in my ear:
Perfume is the rose's child,
But he is born a young man.

(Tension, killing, arrest, ambulance, fire, victims,
accusations, prohibitions, insurrections,
infiltration, interrogation, detention unit,
apprehension, prisons, demolition, occupation),

I said to my imagination, be brave, and put your
    hand on the shoulders of Jerusalem.
And I said to Jerusalem,
I am coming toward you, why do I keep walking backwards?

Translated by Khaled Mattawa

Yael Ben-Israel

GOING IN CIRCLES

So many
I never thought death could undo so many—
I am paraphrasing T.S. Eliot
who is paraphrasing Dante,
walking down a street in downtown Jerusalem;
Stay away from the crowd
cross the road
you never know
what this man might have in his bag,
what this woman might have under her coat
what this person has in mind
every moment, everything
might end with a bang.
No, don't think about it.
Not in this sun
not here, not now!
No, do not fix your eyes before your feet,
look up—
how beautiful
this Unreal City is!

Reja-e Busailah

IN THE SHADOW OF THE HOLY HEIGHTS

for Haniya Suleiman Zarawneh, killed by the Israelis,
at the age of 25, near Jerusalem, January 4, 1988

The sun came out that day from the depth of winter
like the rare orphan of good luck —
what else can the light of heaven be
on a day rising from the dead of winter?

And she had risen before the sun that day
and like her mother and grandmother before her
she washed by hand and wrung by hand
the linen for spouse and child,

and like mother and grandmother
she walked up the wooden ladder
with the pail onto the roof
into the shadow of the Holy Heights —
so clear was the sky
it almost recalled the sight and the scent of the sea down west.

Faithfully she hung her labors on the rope
article by article
that the good sun might dry them for her,
she clasped each with a wooden pin
as safeguard against the prankish wind —

it was no senseless nature that did it when she was done
just about to come down for other chores,
it was no fiendish Nazi,
it was one of the Chosen
selected her heart for his anointed lead
so that limp went the spring in the covenant
which joined soul and limb —

and the good sun shines
and the sheets and the skirts and the nightgowns
and the small socks
and the outfit for the wooden doll
they toss in the wind
and smell like linen hand-washed and sun-dried
they swing lighthearted on the rope
waiting for mother to collect them.

David Gershator

DIVIDING JERUSALEM

In Memoriam: Yehuda Amichai

You take the olives
I'll take the figs
you keep the sparrows
I'll take the doves
you take the red grapes
I'll take the green
divorce divorce
I heard a prophet say
divorce divorce
I heard a young bride weep
is there no other way
you close your roads
I'll open mine
you take the rocks
I'll take the bones
you take the sheep
I'll take the goats
you take the skulls
I'll keep the tombs
fifty-fifty
on the seven gates
Lion's gate for you
Zion gate for me
Omar for you
Moriah for me
we divide Gehenna
we split Siloam's waters
we share Dolorosa
we flip coins
for David's Tower

you take no I take yes
you take yes I take no
divorce divorce
I heard a man calling
to his echo
divorce divorce
I heard the blind
whisper to the deaf
divorce divorce
I heard a widow
talking to the Wall
divorce divorce
a mourner's vow
divorce divorce
an orphan's wail
divorce divorce
you take the voices
I'll hold the visions
you take the tears
I'll hold the cries
you hold the breeze
I'll hold the air
Solomon Solomon
how do we split
this nuclear baby
you take Mohammed's horse
I'll take Messiah's donkey
you take the suras
I'll take the psalms
you beat the durbakee
I'll blast the shofar
you chant Allah hu akbar
I'll sing the Shema
you take the pita
I'll take the matzáh
you make whole
the maimed and crippled

I'll ask Ezekiel
to liven up
wake up
bring back the dead

Naomi Shihab Nye

JERUSALEM

I'm not interested in
Who suffered the most.
I'm interested in
People getting over it.

Once when my father was a boy
A stone hit him on the head.
Hair would never grow there.
Our fingers found the tender spot
and its riddle: the boy who has fallen
stands up. A bucket of pears
in his mother's doorway welcomes him home.
The pears are not crying.
Later his friend who threw the stone
says he was aiming at a bird.
And my father starts growing wings.

Each carries a tender spot:
something our lives forgot to give us.
A man builds a house and says,
"I am native now."
A woman speaks to a tree in place
of her son. And olives come.
A child's poem says,
"I don't like wars,

they end up with monuments."
He's painting a bird with wings
wide enough to cover two roofs at once.

Why are we so monumentally slow?
Soldiers stalk a pharmacy:
big guns, little pills.
If you tilt your head just slightly
it's ridiculous.

There's a place in my brain
Where hate won't grow.
I touch its riddle: wind, and seeds.
Something pokes us as we sleep.

It's late but everything comes next.

Rachel Barenblat

IN THE SAME KEY

They come together to bury their father
in the cave where Sarah's body lies.

(No one imagines the vaulted church
turned mosque with painted ceilings

or the synagogue, or metal detectors
to keep armed men from getting through.)

Isaac and Ishmael wash him with water
and sprinkle sand on his eyelids

so his visions in the world to come
will derive from the land he loved.

Isaac's memories of having a brother
and then losing him without explanation

Ishmael's memories of aching thirst
before his mother saw the spring

go unmentioned, the bones of their past
buried beneath the drifting sands.

Outside the cave the women wail
two families grieving in the same key

not yet the ancestors of enemies
Abraham's dark eyes in every face.

Tawfiq Zayyad

PASSING REMARK

When they ran over her,
the mulberry tree said:
"Do what you wish,
but remember
my right to bear fruit
will never die."

Translated by Sharif Elmusa and Charles Doria

Tawfiq Zayyad

HERE WE WILL STAY

In Lidda, in Ramla, in the Galilee
we shall remain
like a wall upon your chest,
and in your throat
like a shard of glass,
a cactus thorn,
and in your eyes
a sandstorm.

We shall remain
a wall upon your chest,
clean dishes in your restaurants,
serve drinks in your bars,
sweep the floors of your kitchens
to snatch a bite for our children
from your blue fangs.

Here we shall stay,
sing our songs,
take to the angry streets,
fill prisons with dignity.
In Lidda, in Ramla, in the Galilee,
we shall remain,
guard the shade of the fig
and olive trees,
ferment rebellion in our children
as yeast in the dough.

Translated by Sharif Elmusa and Charles Doria

Reuven Goldfarb

SITTING DOWN AT MY COMPUTER ON MOTZAEI SHABBAT

—Parashat VaYishlach—

Icons on my desktop look like tombstones
as I back away from more stories
about the latest Jerusalem bus bombing.

My townspeople go about their tasks
with fallen faces, still absorbing
the details of Thursday morning's massacre.

Despite our charitable deeds,
the grim reality is that murderers,
paid assassins, surface in our midst,

commit their crimes and flee—or are killed—
and, if dead, are feted like celebrities,
if alive, are free to plot and murder again.

The atmosphere is steeped in sadness,
broken only by our festive *Shabbos* joy,
our yearning prayers, plangent melodies,

children's high, harmonious voices,
table talk and courting interludes—
innocent dreams of better days—

and perennial Torah tales, their hidden nuances
revealed in the glare of the headlines:
Jacob, alone, wrestling with—a man?—

becoming Israel, buying land,
journeying again to build an altar,
and keep his promise to the God who rescued him.

19 Kislev, 5763 / November 24, 2002 / Tzfat

Mahmoud Darwish

Excerpt (1): JOURNAL OF AN ORDINARY GRIEF

—Why this arrogance? I have inherited my religion and ethnicity. It was never a question of choice. Now let me ask you, Who among you has chosen to be a Jew? Who?

—This is the difference between you and me. I'm not simply a Jew: I have chosen to be one.

—How?

—The issue is not subject to discussion. Jewishness can be understood only by Jews. That is the source of my pride that you call arrogance.

—I can understand that you have chosen to be a Zionist, or an Israeli. Is that what you mean?

—Not exactly. I mean that I have chosen my Jewishness and have remained faithful to it.

—And how does this faithfulness manifest itself?

—In the historical homeland.

—And what is this historical homeland? Is it vague, like your identity? Have you chosen, or inherited, it?

—It's vague and clear at the same time. I have chosen and inherited it at once.

The speaker was a writer who rebelled against the distinctions that some people drew between Jewishness, Zionism, and Israeliness. He believed that Jewishness can only manifest in Zionism, and Zionism cannot be realized except in Israeliness. From this perspective, renouncing Zionism means forgoing Jewishness. And when you ask him what the historical homeland means in reality, he reminds you of the famous dialogue that took place between Ben-Gurion and an Arab thinker in 1936, when Palestine was still a Zionist dream. When Ben-Gurion was asked what was the "historical homeland," he answered that it was the territory open to Jewish settlement.

— What is the territory?

— The Land of Israel.

— What are its borders?

— The borders of the Land of Israel are known from history.

— Borders are artificial things. They could be here one day, and over there tomorrow.

— The Land of Israel is that which lies between the Mediterranean Sea in the west and the desert in the east, between Sinai in the south and the source of the Jordan in the north.

— You include Transjordan as well?

— Of course. The Jordan is not a border for the Land of Israel. It's a river within the Land of Israel.

Chaim Weizmann used to say, "I know that God promised the Land of Israel to the children of Israel, but I don't know the boundaries allotted by the Lord."

At that time millions of Arabs used to laugh in mockery of Weizmann and Ben-Gurion. When today you consider the secret boundaries "allotted by the Lord" that go beyond Palestine, you realize that "Israeli reality" is "larger than the Zionist dream" and Jewish history, and remember the writer who said to you, "This is the difference between you and me. I'm not simply a Jew: I have chosen to be one."

Will you laugh again, as the Arabs laughed fifty years ago, or will you hand down your dreams to the children born under the bayonets of the Occupation?

Translated by Ibrahim Muhawi

Johnmichael Simon

MORNING AT THE SHUK

Did you notice how plump the avocados are this year
and how perfect, each with its tiny green label of origin
and how the pomegranates are stacked like soldiers
piled crimson with love, quite unlike the Hermon apples
their riotous undisciplined rosy hues
fresh from the Lebanese border smelling of
tractors and mountain air?

Did you pause and watch the children's clothes man
proudly folding T-shirts decorated with the latest
fashionable appliqués rubbing shoulders with
jeans from China and Indian sharwals?
Did you see how carefully the mothers inspect
each garment, checking for hidden flaws or untidy stitching?
Ah yes, I suppose you did.

Did you notice how the herring man
never seems to get older and how red the matjes
looks—probably dyed with beetroot juice?
Did you know that the real shmaltz herring
is hidden in the refrigerator—you have to be
a connoisseur to know that and anyway its
Ramadan month now and mid-morning.

Yet I know why you stopped at the cheese stall
not to let your eyes hunger on fragrant
white and creamy cubes
not to steal an olive from the green or black pile
but because the cheese man works slowly, lovingly,
offering free-taste slivers to undecided housewives
before slipping fragrant portions into heat-sealed bags.

So there was quite a long queue that morning
when you pulled the cord that rocked the market
killing three patient ladies and wounding thirty others
splashing meaty chunks of you over all that white.

Reja-e Busailah

ASMA GOES TO BED WITHOUT SUPPER, A FAIRYTALE

New York Times, 30 March 1988

The tumult about her ruffled the sun
bent on his wheat-colored setting
the air staggered with the echoes
of the sledgehammer smashing open
doors and hollow-hearted glass,
of the throat waxing guttural as it gathered force
to crack a joint or break a collarbone,
of the gasses rising mushroom-like
to wring tears from a dried-up sky;

and she—unnamed by the correspondent of the *New York Times*,
so let her name be Asma—
with seven springs in her heart
barely taller than the wheat in spring
she scarcely started eating her supper
when out of the age of long ago
sprang before her a shape which rage had transformed
into something half human half something else
about which her grandmother had told many a tale.
Before she could shut and open her eyes
as happens in tales of fantasy,
he had snatched up her falafel sandwich
warm and spiced in sunset and sounds of spite.

He did not eat it
though he had a hungry look;
he did not feed it to his children
though all beings feed their children;

50

he did not do with it what his peers and elders did
when they razed her home that they might build a plant,
when they took away her drinking water
that they might fill their swimming pools,
when they raised Hiltons and Sheratons over her
    people's graves.
No! He only snatched up her supper
and tossed it in the gutter with a deep dark grunt—

and Asma stunned in the gathering dark
tearful within the bulldozing of the olive
and the settlement of an alien pine.
Asma, her mother would utter like a seer in the night,
shall be like her namesake, brave Asma
who old and blind and sorrowful
had little doubt that the night shall yet be forced to lift;

better times shall spring out of these times
like in fairytales
and there will be better falafel sandwiches too,
and the Great Judge will forgive her,
her mother would reassure,
the trespass of throwing bread away
and the bread shall follow the man of waste and of the gutter:
it shall dog him forever
and he shall grow hungrier every day.

*Asma was the daughter of Abu-Bakr, the first caliph. Though very old
and blind, she endured with pride and patience the death of her relatives
including her son at the hands of the authorities.*

Tom Berman

THE HATE

The Hate is prowling abroad
It has devoured erstwhile saints
Waxed fat with the souls of sinners
It grows sleek
On the blood
Of passers-by

It is in the mosques and markets,
And in the study halls
Of the righteous settlers

It flies with every stone
Swirling in the smoke of the tires
And the tear gas clouds
It slides satiated
Through the barbed wire

The Hate rides in taxis
To indifferent check posts
On the guarded buses
Climbing lonely country roads
Past the olive groves
Proffering branches of peace

The Hate is warming itself
Behind the shuttered shops
Feeding fat in emergency wards
Smiling at the broken bones
Fractured hopes and shattered lives

The Hate is quite impartial
In a bounteous season
All manner of worshippers
Pay homage
The Hate is come
Into its own country

Shall we let It devour
All our good portion?

Sam Hamod

THERE MUST BE SOMETHING DANGEROUS ABOUT A ZOO IN RAFAH, PALESTINE

Just yesterday, the Israeli tank
came forward, into the zoo,
firing round
after round, the Cockatoos
screeched, the Macaws went
wild in their cages, screen wire
smithering into thousands of
shreds of death, piercing
the 2 AM night air
sending the Raccoon
into panic as his leg
sliced open, and the
Monkey's arm went limp
with the crunch of his tree,
hundreds of Parrots were
caught in a large net
and whisked away in the cab
of the bulldozer, while another
tank shell shattered the
night air, caving in the
roof of the keeper's workshed,
where Mohammad Jumah had
worked for months
creating a zoo
for the children of Rafah, the
only recreation
in this nightmare,
of Israeli destruction,
where children weren't allowed
to go out
fearing Israeli snipers,

old lady Khamis
wanted to stay in her house,
bulldozer grinding toward her,
finally her daughter dragged
her, screaming from the
falling wall that covered them both with
cuts and dust, shattering
memories, creating new
sorrows

But this zoo,
there must have been something dangerous
about this zoo, something
that worried the Israelis, perhaps
it was the smiles
it brought to the children's faces

But now,
"The fox has run off," Jumah says,
but no one has any idea where—probably
dug in behind an old shell hole, shivering
from the shaking ground
as the tank grinds up the last of the
bird enclosures—the bulldozer grabs
and grabs and grabs, pushing
the entire scraps
of the defunct zoo
into the swimming pool

the Macaws cry out
mournfully, covering the
wailing of women,
sobbing of children, the
rage and frustration of Jumah
as he picks up what is left
of the sign that says,
"Welcome to Rafah,
Welcome to our Zoo"

Merle Feld

BIKUR CHOLIM

Before our dialogue today
we are going to visit Najah's brother—
he was shot last week
passing through a checkpoint.

It was dark and raining hard,
he didn't see, didn't hear,
didn't know to stop.
The bullet traveled through
the car door, through
the driver's seat, into
his back, down down
to his spleen.

The soldiers pulled him
from the car,
stripped him naked,
they stood him against a wall,
blood coming from his back,
from his mouth,
in the dark rain
naked.

A passing officer saw,
yelled to the soldiers
Are you crazy?
so they took him
to the military police,
and finally finally,
after double checking
that he had absolutely no record,
to the hospital.

Ten Jewish women — an intifada minyan —
troop through his living room
crowded with friends and neighbors
paying a sick call on Mahmoud,
an ordinary man,
a gentle looking man,
suddenly with many strange women
standing vigil around his bed.

He tells us his story,
in the middle of the telling
his wife rejoins us,
passing a basket
of gaily wrapped candies —
you can't say no,
it would be an insult.
The story is coming to an end.

Slicha, he says, *Slicha* —
it seems that after Mahmoud
engaged an Israeli lawyer
the soldiers came to the hospital
and said *Slicha* —
now you should drop the case —
we said Slicha.

We wish Mahmoud a speedy recovery,
we troop out again through the living room
past the gathering of friends and neighbors —
What? You are not staying for coffee?
No, we can't, we will coffee with
the women of our dialogue group,
today we will talk about
What are Our Sources of Information and
How Do We Know What We Know and
How Do We Decide What is True.

I leave Mahmoud's house and walk
into the gray February muddy sky,
still in the palm of my hand
a gaily wrapped candy.

bikur cholim: (Hebrew) the religious injunction of visiting the sick
slicha: (Hebrew) sorry

Vivien Sansour

LIVE FROM GAZA

Cats nibbling slowly on your flesh
There is all of you to eat and all the time they need
Twenty hours I am watching you bleeding and then
    stop breathing
And in this moment eaten too
Your brother's body next to mine shivering
Losing blood,
Father call 101! Father get an ambulance!
Officer I beg you, I am watching my second son die
    and you can let the ambulance in

"Rady Ani Yaba?"— Are you pleased with me father?
I want to die knowing that you are pleased with me
That the days I made you mad have not stayed with you
That my playfulness never hurt you
That I am in the grace of God a son whose father
    is pleased with him

Forgive me my sons, I screamed, I called all news agencies,
    my voice was even broadcasted on live television
I even pleaded that they would let me try to walk
I would have carried you on my back
The distance between your life and your death
    was only one kilometer
But the distance between my begging and
    the soldier's heart was infinite

And I heard you too father—All the way from Saudi Arabia,
    I saw you and Ibrahim and my other brother
Qassim, I saw you father, you were pleading
You were scraping the gravel with your skin
You were on your knees; your voice was loud and clear
Live from Gaza:

59

"My eldest son just died in front of me, my other son
    is bleeding to death, the ambulance is here, call on
Israeli soldiers to let them in, the hospital is near,
    let me at least walk"

I heard you father you were loud and clear
Sitting in my living room I watched you on live feed
I was one of the millions in their living rooms watching
    the live report from the ground in Gaza
the only difference was
I knew your face, my brother's faces, I recognized
    my brother's left toes as they were photographed like
petrified wood in a forest
I recognized his mole that no one noticed

Live from Gaza father: I saw you between two dead bodies
    and a military commander
Collapsing into tears
Forgive me father, I was in my living room
Forgive me father they would not have let me through
Forgive me father I was over a thousand miles away

And I heard you too father when the phone rang
    all the way from Saudi Arabia to Washington D.C. my
    brother told me
Our brothers are dead
Our father is in hospital
And we are not allowed back in
Live from Gaza: Father I am here in the heart
    of the American capitol
Lobbying senators, calling human rights organizations
Speaking on radio shows, sobbing as I speak
Can I bring Ibrahim back? Can I bring Qassim back?
Can I even be let in to give you a hug from one
    of your remaining sons?
Security reasons
Security reasons

Say that you and I are a security threat
The farm you raised me on is a security threat
My brother's feet
The songs we sing
The cloths we wear, the food we eat, and even our kisses
    are a security threat

Father what do I do here? From the heart of D.C. I cannot
    even swim from this shore to the Mediterranean Sea
I am a security threat father
My loss could make me angry
My loss could make me mad
My loss father could make me crazy
My loss father could make me into a terrorist

I throw my diplomas and certificates away
Father, I never belonged here and when the good people
    of this land come to hold me they say: "I am so sorry
    about your loss"
What do I say father? Which loss? My brothers? Your tears?
    Or the heart that has been carved into pieces?
Father, I answer them, I say: "I know you are good people"
I want to stay faithful to what I was taught
Treat people with respect
But father I am a security threat
My respect, my lack of respect, the mere fact that I am
    from Gaza father
Negates the fact that I am the son of a farmer
The son of a fisherman, the humble man of the sea
My identity father is a Gazan and when people look at me
They judge me with the lies they know
Palestine does not exist
Palestine is not a country and your people are angry people
Why do you hate us so much?

Live from Gaza: nothing has changed.
I have been released from the hospital but my two sons are
    dead and the other two are in exile.

Ellen Bass

MOONLIGHT

On the radio, Amer Shurrab tells how
his father and two brothers were stopped in Gaza
by Israeli soldiers. Both brothers shot.
One dead on one side of the car.
One bleeding to death on the other—
twenty hours in his father's arms
while soldiers wouldn't let a medic through.
Maybe there shouldn't have been moonlight
shining on this father as he crawled
behind the car, driving off the feral cats
skulking around his son's body.
Maybe this is no place for the dignity
of the physical world, its constancy.
The moon waxes full, glazing the crown
of the father's head, the planes and angles
of his sons' faces. You can see it reflected
in the dark pools of their blood.

Yasmin Snounu

INSIDE THE FLAME OF THE CAST LEAD

Friday, January 16, 2009

Yesterday, from the first hours of the twentieth day of war,
my family and I were the closest we've come to death;
the Israeli army pinpointed its barbarous operation
on Gaza City's Tal El Hawa neighborhood, where we live.

F16s, tanks and artillery continuously shelled,
launching phosphorous bombs whose smoke
carried poisonous gas into the houses.

The Al Amany building, where I live with my family and
    my uncle's family—
who left their house which was damaged when F16s
    bombed the ministerial compound—
got its portion of devastation; many phosphorous bombs
    hit it,
and an Israeli tank shelled the fourth floor.

Our parents kept trying to calm my terror-stricken siblings,
    who were panicking;
they prevented us from looking out the windows.
Their voices still shake in my mind when I remember them
    saying
"Keep away from the windows," the apartment was also
    shaking the whole time.

I stole moments away from my parents' distraught time
    and captured a few pictures.
Much of what happened will remain untold because
    outsiders couldn't reach the area;
even reporters and ambulances didn't manage to get near
    the tumultuous destruction.

I tried again and again to take closer looks, but couldn't
make out what I needed to see.

Brave men were saving their family members,
jumping over phosphorous fireballs that were everywhere.
Phosphorous bombs had set their house on fire.
A man went on the roof to put water on the fire,
then the F16 shot him too while he tried to put out the fire.
He was injured and after a while another man
      of the same family
came along driving a bulldozer with its scoop full of sand.
He tried to pour it onto the fire, but the Israeli plane shot
another phosphorous bomb to prevent him from dousing
      the fire.

I was astonished by our neighbor's courage;
even though he was hit by one of those bombs,
he still continued putting sand on the fire,
At the same time that another man was trying to evacuate
the children, women and an old grandfather and grandmother,
the man driving the bulldozer was also covering
      the way for them.

Watching our neighbors die right in front of us,
we have never been this close to death.
Our water tanks were also damaged by phosphorous bombs
shot helter-skelter everywhere. We managed to vacate

our apartment and go to another house in Al Zaitoon
but things were worse there, so we went to
      our grandfather's house.

The catastrophic humanitarian situation keeps deteriorating.
People die from the Israeli attack, or lack of medicine,
      water and food.
Gazans try to survive by cooking with wood from
      the remains of their houses.

Although NGOs have sent some food to Gaza, it is still not enough.

Um Azmi, a Gazan woman who suffers severely when cooking or
making tea and coffee,
has to salvage and burn wood from her house to have heat for
cooking.
Her balcony wall is blackened from the smoke of burning wood.
She and her family have had to breathe in harmful smoke so she can
feed her children.
Today, while I photographed her as she cooked,
she confirmed that we were back in a primitive epoch.

Johnmichael Simon

WATERS OF GAZA

June 22, 2009

They moved out of Gaza
not without protest, not without prayer
feeling like ivy ripped off the walls
like irrigation pipes torn from the soil
they moved out on unwilling legs
on buses to nowhere
fathers, mothers, children
and children without fathers
without mothers

They moved into Gaza
not without covet, not without envy
feeling like water released from a dam
bursting into surrendering fields
carrying all before it, trees, houses
places of prayer, fences, gardens
waves breaking over alien temples
again and again till water covered all

After the water came briny hatred
lusting for a redder liquid
and the skies darkened again
lightening and thunder returned to Gaza
rained on this thin strip of unhappiness
writhing between the wrath of history
and the dark depths of the sea

Richard Tillinghast

WHAT IS NOT ALLOWED

No toys are allowed, no tinned meat, no tomato paste,
no clothing, no shoes, no notebooks,
no sewing machines or spare parts for sewing machines.
These will be stored in our warehouses at Kerem Shalom
until further notice.

Bananas, apples, and persimmons are allowed into Gaza,
peaches and dates, and now macaroni
(after the American Senator's visit).
These are vital for daily sustenance.
But no apricots, no plums, no grapes, no avocados, no jam.
These are luxuries and are not allowed.
Paper for textbooks is not allowed.

The terrorists could use it to print seditious material.
And why do you need textbooks
now that your schools are rubble?
No steel is allowed, no building supplies, no plastic pipe.
These the terrorists could use to launch rockets
against us.

Pumpkins and carrots you may have,
but no delicacies,
no cherries, no pomegranates, no watermelon, no onions,
no chocolate, no coffee beans.

We have a list of three dozen items that are allowed,
but we are not obliged to disclose its contents.
This is the decision arrived at
by Colonel Levi, Colonel Rosenzweig, and Colonel Segal.
Our motto:
'No prosperity, no development, no humanitarian crisis.'

You may fish in the Mediterranean,
but only as far as three km from shore.
Beyond that and we open fire.
It is a great pity the waters are polluted –
twenty million gallons of raw sewage dumped into the sea every day
is the figure given.
Our rockets struck the sewage treatments plants,
and at this point spare parts to repair them are not allowed.

As long as Hamas threatens us,
no cement is allowed, no glass, no medical equipment.
We are watching you from our pilotless drones
as you cook your sparse meals over open fires
and bed down
in the ruins of houses destroyed by tank shells.

And if your children can't sleep,
missing the ones who were killed in our incursion,
or cry out in the night, or wet their beds
in your makeshift refugee tents,
or scream, feeling pain in their amputated limbs –
that's the price you pay for harboring terrorists.

God gave us this land.
A land without a people for a people without a land.

Rachel Barenblat

FIRST VISIT TO THE CAMP D'HAISHA, BETHLEHEM

There are no canvas tents.
The buildings don't look
so bad, standard-issue
developing-world
cement block structures

until I try to imagine
eleven thousand people
in one square kilometer,
one in every minyan
an angry alumnus

of the Israeli jails.
What do I know
about settlers or rock-throwers,
one state, two state
impossibilities?

But our grandparents
didn't escape the ghettos
of Europe's worst era
only to create new ones
for somebody else.

When we depart
I'm saddened, troubled
but perfectly able
to order a cold beer
and make conversation.

The sorrow and the fury
dormant overnight
explode the next day.
Even Shabbat can't soothe
my lacerated heart.

Lahab Assef Al-Jundi

HOLY LANDERS

Listen!
You are fighting over a land that can fit,
with wilderness to spare,
in the Panhandle of Texas.

You are building walls to segregate,
splitting wholes till little is left,
killing and dying for pieces of sky
in the same window.

The olive trees are dying
of embarrassment.
They have enough fruits
and pits for all of you.
All they want is for you to stop
uprooting them.
Sending your children to die
in their names.

Listen!
Your land is no holier than my backyard.
None of you is any more *chosen*
than the homeless veteran panhandling
with a *God Bless* cardboard sign
at the light of Mecca
and San Pedro.

Draw a borderline around the place.
Call it home for all the living,
all the dead,
all the tired exiles with its dust
gummed on their tongues.

There are no heroes left.

Doreen Stock

GIRL'S BURIAL/GAZA 2009

Patriotism anarchism
martyrdom the swift kiss
of your older sister death
with blackbird eyes and feathered
hair swept back beyond tribal windsong
her penciled eyebrow arching into sky
who has come to bury you
not here, no,
but tucking the bright orange cloth around
you from the very bolt of silk the arms
were wrapped in, the Chinese Russian American Israeli
British Iranian arms that fall out and let you, warm little
cartilage elbow and throat, two knees one with scab on it
toes curled hands slightly clenched curly dark brown hair
still damp around your quiet face, let you fall in, not an
engine of destruction, saying with your silence to every
arms dealer in this war game grown up and mad:
WHY DIDN'T YOU
BUY MY LIFE INSTEAD?

COME TO BURY YOU IN SKY, TREE, STAR,
LANDSCAPE AGAINST THIS WAR FOREVER. Amen.

Fadwa Tuqan

I SHALL NOT WEEP

for the Poets of the Resistance, on our meeting in Haifa

My loved one, at the gate of Jaffa,
in the chaos of rubble and thorns,
I stood and spoke to my own eyes:
  Let us cry for those who've abandoned
  their demolished homes.
The houses call for their owners,
announcing their deaths.

The heart said:
  What have the troubles done to you, homes,
  and where are your inhabitants —
  have you received any news of them?
  Here where they used to be, and dream,
  and draw their plans for the morrow —
  Where's the dream and the future now?
  And where have they gone?
The rubble stayed silent.
Nothing spoke but the absence.
  I shall not weep
And the silence of silences . . .
  strange flocks of phantom owls
  hovered over the place,
  becoming the new masters.
Oh, how the heart was wrung with grief!

Dear ones!
I wiped the grey cloud of tears off my eyelids
to meet you, eyes shining with love and faith
  in you, in the land, in man
What shame it would be to meet you
  with trembling eyelids,

73

a dampened heart full of despair.
Now I am here to borrow fire from you,
to borrow from your lit lamps lighting
    the blackness—
a drop of oil for my own.
I stretch my hand to yours
    and raise my brow to the sun beside you.
If you are strong as mountain stones
and fresh as the sweet flowers of our land,
how can a wound destroy me?
And how could I ever cry in front of you?
I make my pledge:
    From this day forward I shall not cry!

Dear ones, our nation's steed has transcended
    yesterday's fall!
Beyond the river, hear the confident neigh
    of the risen stallion,
listen! Shaking off the siege of darkness,
galloping towards his anchor on the sun!
Processions of horsemen gather
    to bless him,
to bid him drink from their crimson blood,
to feed him from their limbs and sinews.
They address the free stallion:
Run towards the eye of the sun!
Run, oh stallion of our people,
visible symbol and banner,
we are the army behind you,
the tide of our anger will not recede.
We shall not rest till
    the shadows are dispelled.

Lamps of the dark night,
    brothers in the wound,
sweet secret of yeast
    and scattered seeds of wheat

that die in your giving . . .
on your road I shall walk.
In the light of your eyes
I collect yesterday's tears
  and wipe them away.
Like you, I plant my feet on the land,
  my country,
and fix my eyes, like yours,
  on the road of light and sun.

Translated by Naomi Shihab Nye and Salma Khadra Jayyusi

Rochelle Mass

HANDS ON A GUN

The soldier has slipped on my shoulder again, his breath skips
with the road. His head falls to my chest, I straighten, tightening
the part of my back that usually goes sore on rides long as this.
His knee hits mine, then flips away as the bus rolls, returns
to mine, stays there. I feel his muscles.

Hills are drying in the June sun. Goats and two camels pass
on my side and dark children sell eggplants from plastic crates.
The soldier's head falls almost into my arms, I lift his face.
His hands stay on the gun,
a scar goes from the thumb up the arm. Swollen and red.

The bus makes a sharp turn. The low area between the hills
is filled with black tents; wide women herd sheep and children to
grass left after winter. The soldier has slipped again.
I lift his face, saliva runs on my hand,
then I touch his hair.

The bus stops.
Three soldiers push duffel bags in.
The last eats cherries, spits out the stones.
An old lady with parsley in her lap shouts at him,
the next stone rolls under her skirt.

The bus revs up and my soldier boy shakes himself
like a dog out of water.
Shalom he says to me.
Shalom I say and feel the sweat
I took each time I raised his head.

Where are we?
He leans over to see more tents and goats.
Almost there?
He asks and answers
long way yet.

I want to look straight at him but study
his hands on the gun, want to know if he's afraid.
There's so much more I want to say
but you can't talk like
that to a man you hardly know.

Vivien Sansour

A LETTER FROM AN ISRAELI SOLDIER TO HIS MOTHER

Moving into Gaza
No Fighters here
A loud question bursts in my chest: What am I doing here?

They say I must fulfill my duties to protect my people
My people are at a shopping mall
Consuming—the new opium of the masses

No fighters here
I am panicked
I had never seen their faces before
Palestinians
Those creatures behind the wall
I had never seen their faces before
What do I do here?

The little girl paralyzed stuck to the ground like
    a wounded rabbit
I looked at her
I just killed your mother
Your father and your brother's son

What am I doing here?
I wonder as I celebrate our "triumph" in the Gaza strip
Her eyes haunt me
The little girl
I don't know her name
Better not to
It would be worse if I did

I must celebrate
My commander is here
He says: proud of your hard work!
Ehud Olmert assures me: We will protect each one of you
    from such allegations
War crimes nonsense

No war crimes here
Just a polite request
Lady with the 10 children
We have come into your home
"Choose which five of your children you want to give
    as a gift to Israel"
You don't want to choose?
We will choose for you
I chose two and Yosi chose the other three
We shot them dead in front of her eyes

No war crimes here
Good job
We are proud of you
And the question keeps trying to pass through
    the checkpoints of my mind
The security walls of my heart that shot a child
What am I doing here?

We are only defending ourselves
These children grow up to be suicide bombers
I am just following orders
No war crimes here
And a lingering question
What did I do there?
What am I doing here?
The sound of a woman crying
A moving limb from under the rubbles
And a dead human body made dinner for dogs
White phosphorus and nerve gas

No war crimes here I am just protecting my people
From Arabs who eat with their hands
No war crimes here, mother,
I just killed a woman and her child won't stop crying

Gloria Bletter

NO SAFE SKY

> Peace is a sea
> whose waves
> will carry us far.
>
> —*Ella Bat-Tzion*

I meant to think drums
    and thought bombs,
I meant to dream land
    and dreamt land-mines,
I meant to hear thunder
    and heard tanks rolling,
I meant to see lightning
    and saw burning bursts of white gas
    and searchlights scanning the night.

They warned of a place full of terrorists,
I said they must mean *full of terror*—

    in the eyes of the children,
    in their frantic games
    their paintings of dead men and homes
        without walls
    their running back and forth, trying to hide
        from the sky
    in their folded paper machine guns, gripped
        by small hands and pointed heavenward,

and in the fast beats of their hearts.

And those mothers, teachers: I saw
wary eyes, heard words of worry—
        not only for the maiming of the young
        but for fear that fear will grow up to hate

And all, visitors and wounded, ask:
Will more hate come
along the green-blue line,
along the beige beaches,
fronting a sunny Mediterranean sea?

Reja-e Busailah

ALI OF LYDDA

Before the conqueror shot him dead
from the top of our roof,
he had on his head
as he walked homeward in the morning sun
a tray made of straw and of circles,
none vicious though:
each flowed into the next
from small to large to larger rounds:

the first bore the transformation
of the dream of wheat, its ears still close to the ground,
into loaves of exciting breath;
the second of a humble communion
of young and old breaking bread into lasting bond
under the sanctity of one roof;
the third of modest hopes
which rose and tossed like one vast field shedding green
in the wind and ripening sun;
the fourth of a dream beyond,
half formed, half grasped —

after he shot him dead
and the tray fell in manner undignified
and the bread tumbled and scattered
on hot hard stone
in shapes of heads rolling about a sanctuary,
I heard the conqueror on the high roof
under the bare sky,
I heard him snort
I heard him spit on the ground
I heard him piss
through the eye of light.

Rochelle Mass

FROM MY KITCHEN WINDOW

I often think there's a woman on the hill
over there, who looks out her kitchen window
in my direction
as she prepares dinner for her family.

Perhaps that woman has watched our village grow.
Perhaps
she's seen it spread over the Gilboa
new homes built for young families
children playing in the yard.

I watch Jenin stretch so wide
I have to turn my head
each way
to see the full size of it.

Perhaps that woman is picking olives, as I am
soaking them in large bins then
slicing lemons, adding coarse salt
tossing in bay leaves, peppercorns and

sharp red peppers to get the right flavor. Perhaps
she helps her husband, as I help mine
take their crop to the local press, return
with gallons of oil.

I watch evening stagger over Jenin as
I soap my dishes
see lights splash
over the city.

I wonder if that woman
is looking my way –
I would ask if she's angry
if she's afraid.

Erik Sutter-Kaye

AHL AL-KITAB

In my Jewish family
I am a Palestinian.

I am the eldest son.
Call me Ishmael.

Actually, my parents named me Jesus.
My Hebrew name was his; pronounced: *Ii-say*

No one remembers why they named me his,
But look what they did to him.

I had what my family wanted and they took it:
Palestine had what the refugees wanted and they took it:

My mother and father fought their battles through me
The holocaust survivors fought their war on G-d
on the West Bank

No one protected me so I must have deserved it
The nations who turned down Jewish immigrants
    did not protect the PLA

Both my parents and the Zionists were intensely
    victimized in Europe
How could they ever possibly become victimizers?

I love my family but I left them.
Ahl al-Kitab — "the People of the Book"
What do you do when the children of the prophet
refuse to see?

Yousef el Qedra

I HAVE NO HOME

I saw clouds running away from the hurt.
I have no language.
Its weight is lighter than a feather.
The quill does not write.
The ink of the spirit burns on the shore of meaning.
The clouds are tears, filled with escape and lacking definition.
A cloud realizes the beauty she forms —
beauty which contains all good things,
for whom trees, gardens, and tired young women wait.

I have no home.
I have a night overripe with sweats caused by numbness all over.
Time has grown up on its own without me.
In my dream, I asked him what he looks like.
My small defeats answered me.
So I asked him again, What did he mean?
Then I found myself suspended in nothingness,
stretched like a string that doesn't belong to an instrument.
The wind played me. So did irresistible gravity.
I was a run of lost notes that have a sad, strong desire to live.

June 22, 2009

Translated by Yasmin Snounu and Edward Morin

Elana Bell

ON A HILLTOP AT THE NASSAR FARM IN THE WEST BANK OVERLOOKING THE SURROUNDING SETTLEMENT OF NEVE DANIEL

I am writing this poem for Amal,
whose name means *hope*,
who thinks of each tree she's planted like a child,
whose family has lived in the same place
for a hundred years, and when I say place
I mean this exact patch of land
where her father was born, and his father,
so that the shoots he planted before her birth
now sweep over her head. Every March
she plucks the green almonds and chews
their sour fuzzy husks like medicine.

How can I write a poem for someone
whose family refuses to leave?

I am from a people who move,
who crossed sea and desert and cities
with stone monuments, with clocks, with palaces,
on foot, on skeleton trains, through barracks
with iron bunks, aching for a place we could stay.
All our prayers, all our songs for that place
where we had taken root once, where we had been
the ones to send the others packing and now—

Amal laughs with all her teeth and her feet
tickle the soil when she walks. She moves
through her land like an animal. She knows it
in the dark. She feeds stalks to the newborn

colt and collects its droppings like coins
to fertilize the field. Amal loves this land
and when I say land I mean this
exact dirt and the fruit of it
and the sheep who graze it and the children
who eat from it and the dogs who protect it
and the tiny white blossoms it scatters in spring.

And when I say love, I mean Amal has never married.

All around her land the settlements sprout like weeds.
They block out the sun and suck precious water
through taps and pipes while Amal digs wells
to collect the rain. I am writing this poem
though I have never drunk rain
collected from a well dug by my own hands,
never pulled a colt through
the narrow opening covered in birth fluid
and watched its mother lick it clean,
or eaten a meal made entirely of things
I got down on my knees to plant.

And when I say settlement I mean
I love the red tiled roofs,
the garden in the shape of a garden,
water that comes when I call it forth
with the flick of my wrist and my hand on the tap.
Only lately I find that when I ache
it takes the shape of a well.
And when I bleed I emit a scent
something like a sheep in heat,
like dirt after rain,
like a patch of small white flowers
too wild to name.

Peter Marcus

DIALOG BENEATH THE LIGHT

A Collage of Lines from Mahmoud Darwish and Yehuda Amichai

Where is the road
to the road?

Here,
underneath the kites that children are flying.

You who stand in the doorway, come in . . .
Come in, and sip with us our Arabic coffee.

In the garden, at the white table,
two dead men were sitting in the midday heat.

Drink a glass of juice . . . Munch an apple . . .
pour out wine into two glasses . . .

Each year the melons
are sweeter than the year before.

In the elegy of the phoenix
I can't tell my ashes apart from your dust.

Must I . . . sleep among rocks . . . camouflage my love with worries . . .
live underground like a mole.

History . . . has no rest stops . . . for us
to look toward what time has done to us.

I escaped once and don't remember what god it was from, what test.
So I'm floating inside my life, like Jonah in his dark fish.

The exile tells himself: "If I were a bird
I would burn my wings."

Now I am no longer I ,
and you no longer you.

Where should we go after the last border. Where should we go
    after the
last sky?

I don't imagine on the night of the exodus from Egypt,
between midnight and dawn, any couple could lie together in love.

We travel like everyone else,
but return to nothing.

My life is being blotted out behind me according to a precise map.
How much longer can those memories hold out?

We store our sorrows in our jars . . .
We store them for other seasons.

Other people's memories cling to me
like dogs.

We have other tasks besides searching
for graves and elegies.

Too many dead, too little
earth to cover them all.

At least save us one wall for our laundry lines, and one
night for songs.

Spilled blood is not the roots of trees
but it's the closest thing to roots we have.

Can people be born of
a guillotine?

Perhaps Jerusalem is a dead city
with people swarming like maggots.

I wish the sky
was real (a man passing between two bombs told me.)

I lift up my eyes to the hills. Now I understand
what it means to lift up the eyes, what a heavy burden it is.

When the fighter planes disappear, the doves fly
white, white. Washing the sky's cheek with free wings.

And what's the difference between
my sky and your land?

. . . The questions that are asked in these hills are the same
*   as they've always been.*
"Have you seen my sheep?" "Have you seen my shepherd?'

Don't ask the trees for their names.
Don't ask the valleys who their mother is.

And I won't even mention
the crying of orphans.

When life becomes normal we'll grieve like others
over personal matters that bigger headlines have kept hidden.

Before God closes his hand . . .
before we have nowhere to stand.

I have lived on the land long before swords
turned man into prey.

A soldier is filling bags with soft sand
he used to play in

91

When I searched his pockets for a name, I found two photographs,
one of his wife and the other of his daughter.

God's hand is in the world
like my mother's hand in the guts of a slaughtered chicken.

I guided my son to my grave,
he liked it and slept there, without saying goodbye.

Grief is a very heavy board,
tears are nails.

He told me about the moment of departure, how his mother
silently wept when they led him to the front.

The pain-people think God is the God of joy,
the joy-people think God is the god of pain.

I know what it means when the dove
lays its eggs on the rifle's muzzle . . .

My heart was covered in dreams
like my shiny shoes covered with dust.

A mother sees in her son's eyes
the fear the carnation harbors for the vase.

Listen my son . . . When you go out on night patrol fill your canteen
to the top so the water won't make a sloshing sound and give you away.
That's how your soul ought to be in your body, large and full and silent,
(When you make love, make all the noise you want.)

I love the particles of sky that slip through the skylight—
    a meter of light
where horses swim.

God is hiding,
and man cries Where have you gone.

Nothing takes me away from the butterfly of my dreams . . .
    a bird
welcoming the dawn on an olive branch.

Between a dead man and his mourner I'll start living from now
    on and wait there
as it grows dark . . . I have nothing to say about the war, nothing
    to add. I'm ashamed.

I dreamed the earth's heart is greater
than its map.

And he who was lost like a dog will be found
like a human being and brought back home again.

Salaam is the lament of a young man whose heart
a woman's beauty mark pierced, not a bullet or a bomb.

I believe with perfect faith . . . at this very moment millions
    of human being are standing at
crossroads and intersections . . . showing each other where
    to turn, what the right way is.

Where
is the road to the road?

I touch your mouth that now, perhaps,
will sing.

You will carry me and I will carry you.
Strangers are also brothers.

When a man's far away from his country for a long time,
his language becomes more precise, more pure.

Share my bread, drink my wine,
don't leave me alone like a tired willow.

Susan Martin

GLOBAL WARMING

My husband, a born extrovert,
tried small talk as an ice breaker.
Do you own this shop, he asked
the shopkeeper, or do you rent it?

Ninety degrees outside on the Via Dolorosa,
inside the trinket shop North Pole frigid.

Sir, he replied, *I do not own this shop,*
nor do I rent it. I am a teacher.
I do not make enough money
to support my family, so I must
supplement my income by working here.

Really, I said. *I'm a teacher, too.*

Call it detente; call it global warming.
No longer were we Jew and Muslim,
American and Arab,
Zionist and Palestinian nationalist.
We were colleagues with a common enemy.

Together over steaming cups of coffee,
we did what teachers do best,
bitch, bitch, bitch.

Tawfiq Zayyad

BEFORE THEIR TANKS

On my window sill
rose petals bloomed
From the grapevine sprang
an arbor, a green
ladder
And my house leaned
against a bundle
of sunrays and bathed.
That was before their tanks
came.

THEY KNOW

But they know that my country
has known a thousand conquerors
and they know
that the thousand
have all melted away
like driven snow.

Translated by Sharif Elmusa and Charles Doria

Tawfiq Zayyad

SALMAN

Before a bomb buried
him in his courtyard
Salman told us:

"Loved ones,
for a long time we did not live
the way we wanted:
now we do!"

Translated by Sharif Elmusa and Charles Doria

Sandy Polishuk

POSSESSION

They thought if they just went there and stayed there and
kept saying it was theirs that it would be so Miriam Levinger
the rabbi's wife took her children and six other women some
of them were pregnant too and their children and they had
many children at least forty among them and together at three
o'clock in the morning they snuck into the old Hadassah
hospital in the middle of Hebron where sixty-seven Jews
were massacred in '29 and had been *Judenrein* since the
last anti-Jewish riot in '36 when the British evacuated the
remnants of the community so it was especially important
to be there except the government was ambivalent because
they wanted the whole of the land too especially this city
with its long history King David's first capital the cave where
Abraham and Sarah are buried but they knew it would be
hard to rotect settlers so they hoped if it was difficult enough
Miriam and the others would give up and go home so they
wouldn't let them bring their furniture and there wasn't any
water or plumbing and they couldn't go out to shop for food
because if they left the army wouldn't let them return so their
husbands brought food and water and put it in the baskets
the women lowered from the windows high above the street
and they slept on the floor and the children had a holiday
from school and after awhile when the women didn't give in
the government did so the women made it a nice home with
beds and tables and washing machines and refrigerators and
husbands and the army came and built them toilets and even
moved in on the top floor and Miriam was happy victorious
but the people of the city were furious and killed one of their
young men a student so the government retaliated blew up
houses then voted to let more settlers come to other buildings
but that made the people of the city even angrier so on Friday
night they threw grenades and shot rifles as the Yeshiva boys

returned from services at the Tomb of the Patriarchs their
white shirts gleaming as they walked down the dark street
and six of the boys lay dead and then bombs went off in
cars of Arab mayors and everything kept escalating as the
government remodeled apartments in five old buildings and
subsidized the rent of the new settlers and when Miriam who
is a nurse was called to tend a man who had been stabbed
she thought he was an Arab and so she walked away maybe
nurses don't take the Hippocratic oath and he died and her
side hates their side and their side hates her side and now
there are four hundred Jews living in the Arab's city and
even with three soldiers for every settler can the government
protect them because even though Miriam was victorious and
lives in the city she wasn't able to stop the peace process but
she will stay calling on ancient history and saying that the
Bible is their deed since this land was promised to them and
everyone knows that but what of the others who are there
who will stay there too no matter how badly they are treated
because they too believe it belongs to them and so it is that
often two people or two peoples are both right even though
what they say is at opposite poles and no one who is outside
of it can understand it is like being friends with both people
in the middle of a nasty divorce only with a divorce there is
an end

Author's Note:
The statistic of the number of Jews living in Hebron was accurate
when this poem was written in 1997.

Nizar Qabbani

AN INVITATION FOR THE FIFTH OF JUNE

(on the fifth anniversary of the Arab defeat in June 1967)

You come back for the fifth year,
barefoot, a burlap sack slung on your back,
the sadness of the heavens mapped on your face —
so, too, the pain of Job,
and we'll greet you at every airport
with bouquets, and drink your health with copious wine.
We'll sing and recite insincere poems in your presence,
and you'll get used to us
and we to you.

*

We ask you to vacation here in summer,
like all tourists,
and we'll designate you the royal suite
prepared especially for you.
You may enjoy the night . . . and the neon lights,
the rock and roll, the porno and the jazz —
here we know only felicity,
and in my country you'll find what pleases,
furnished flats for lovers,
abundance of liquor,
and a harem for the caliph.

Why are you so curtailed in flight?
My sad-faced guest,
we have streams and grass and beautiful girls,
so why your diffidence?
We'll help you forget Palestine,
and pluck the tear-tree from your eyes,

and from the Qur'an erase the verses,
    the "Compassionate" and the "Conquest,"
and we'll assassinate Jesus Christ
and grant you an Arab passport
that has no return visa.

*

Fifth year
sixth
seventh
eighth
ninth
tenth year
what do the years amount to?
All our grand cities, from the Euphrates to the Nile,
are lost now to memory.
We've forgotten the men who disappeared in the desert
and those who died are extinguished.
What do the years count for?
We've prepared the funeral wreaths and the scarves
and composed the orations,
and carved, a week before your arrival,
the marble of the tombstones.
O East that feeds on the paper of communiques
and trails like a lamb behind posters
O East that writes the name of its fallen
on the faces of mirrors
on the waists of belly dancers —
what do the years count for?
What ever do they amount to?

Translated by Sharif Elmusa and Jeremy Reed

C.B. Follett

PALESTINE

Persians
  Romans
    Ottoman Turks
     British
      Jordanians
       Israelis

      He had a gun
It was a stick   He aimed at us
his mother's broom   It was black
It was black   He wanted it to be a gun
He was seven

   Here is his blood.

I'm good with a rock
         It's tough duty
Just a little Palestinian David
         They're good with rocks
right between the eyes
         the windshield crazed
aim right and things happen
         his jeep went off the cliff.

We used to be neighbors
         we don't speak
worked together, borrowed
         stay on our side of the road

He can't help me
                    nothing we can do.
          Collaborator!

I want to go to school
                    All classes are canceled
there are no jobs
                    and they want our jobs
I want to write poetry
                    they are rabble
It's lonely, I'm empty
                    always making trouble

I am someone
                    I am someone.

We can't go out at night
                    We must have curfew
it presses like iron grates
                    for your safety
There are fourteen in my family
                    no more than ten may gather
so our house was bulldozed
                    there must be rules.

Tell me, are there still stars?

Samuel Hazo

INTIFADA

Singly at first, then doubly
  then slowly by the tens or twenties,
  then steadily on . . .
                    Interviewed
  about the deathcount in Ramallah,
  one sergeant said, "We'll kill
  them all, but we'll never
  forgive them for making us do it."
Later he aimed his Uzi at a boy
  armed with a stone and a slingshot,
One general claimed his soldiers
  fired only rubber-coated bullets.
When asked about the difference
  to the dead, he frowned and shouted,
  "Their leaders and parents use
  these children as human shields."
Despite the contradicting photographs,
  pundits and lobbyists concurred.
After all, who could deny
  that boys with all their lives
  ahead of them would happily
  seek execution, that mothers loved
  to see their sons in open
  coffins, that choosing a brave
  death instead of a lifelong one
  was an option for fools?
                    No one
  would claim that occupation
  to the occupied resembled daily
  suffocation.
                    No one would add
  that suffocation or the fear of it

begot a courage born
of desperation.
No one compared it
to the fate of being locked
in darkness in a stalled elevator
underground. Like someone buried
upright and alive, anyone
trapped there would stop at nothing.

Judy Kronenfeld

THIS WAR

On my car radio, NPR reports the funeral,
at Jerusalem's military cemetery, of a soldier
killed in the fight with Hezbollah.
His classmate, speaking in lilting
English, sounding philosophical, praises the dead
boy's love of hiking, love of country, ultimate
gift; his uncle says his nephew understood
the war was a matter of his country's life
or death; his commanding officer — translated
matter-of-factly, and roundly, as if
giving a recipe — praises his modesty
and enthusiastic participation, and I feel how
repeated and repeated and made ordinary
by repetition these gestures are, until —

from another planet, his mother's voice
rises from the wellspring
of pure grief, and I hear grief thickening
her Hebrew, so that even the flat
translation vibrates with it
My Yonatan, my Yonatan
my own tears spring with hers
I have loved you from the moment
you were born
and the windshield blurs.

I think of my own grown
American children, and my stomach
clenches, Stop!

Yet there is this brief, strange
exaltation of pain ascending through

the ceiling of the day into rarer air,
an exaltation of being pulled up short
by the ultimate, a terrible Hollywood aura
of war movie glamour, that deadens
the boredom of the quotidian —
the boredom of my current run
to the supermarket for orange juice
and a Rotisserie chicken for dinner . . .
a tiny bitter nub of attraction
I squint my eyes against
and rub out.

It can't be that luxurious frisson —
can it? — that makes a mother say "I'm not sad
about my kids. Now they're martyrs
in heaven?" That makes a dry-eyed
commanding officer approve
the sacrifice of youth? Powerlessness
or pride then, propaganda? The romance
of a meaningful death must be so brief.
I roll my cart past robust vegetables
refreshed with mist and remember
reading what that Lebanese
mother first said — her tongue
dust-heavy in the galloping dust of Qana:
she heard one of the babies
pinned against her back in the rubble
cry, but she couldn't move;
she thought Fatima and Roqaya,
still warm, still lived . . .

Here, I leave the clear and beautiful
aisles, I take home my cold, clean
orange juice, so sweet in a dusty
throat, my glistening chicken
dripping into its plastic pan,

though I am ashamed
to love them because Yonatan's mother cries,
because there is only dust
in Qana, because my own children
are so safe, for now,
on an American coast.

Mahmoud Darwish

Excerpt (2): JOURNAL OF AN ORDINARY GRIEF

He Who Kills Fifty Arabs Loses One Piaster . . .

Here they lie. Their names were many, and their death was one. They were tired, and sunset came quickly.

They fell to the ground with ease and without saying anything because the appointed time had come suddenly. What if they had been told? They knew what was required. The whole family was returning home from work, but the world was not for them.

Here they lie. They were punished for an obscure crime. They did not take part in a demonstration, and did not defend life and soil except with prayer. They used to leave their misery early in the morning, and return to it before sunset. They were waiting for rain, but death fell on them like a heavy rain.

Here they sleep. The sunset grows larger and changes into forests of dry trees. There is no hour to commemorate their death, no occasion, and no appointment. The stones themselves are time, and the expanse of the pale sunset is time. What name shall we give them?

The Kufr Qasem Massacre is not a day for remembrance, and it is not a passing phase that forgetfulness will defeat. It is rather the history of a hatred that began from the moment Herzl drew his sword out of the Torah and brandished it in the face of the Orient. The inhabitants of this down-trodden and neglected village did not engage in anything that should rouse anyone's anger, even the ones who had volunteered to be the enemy. They fought only against harsh nature and black despair. Why then did they die? They did not die for our sake at all. They were victims, not martyrs. And that is their twofold tragedy, and the source of our twofold grief over them.

We could say that they died so that our hatred of oppression and usurpation would grow deeper and our worship of the land would deepen. We do not need such savage facts. We are perfectly capable of developing our sense of love or hatred without this death for nothing. For what did they die then?

Not for our sake but for that of the killers, so that Zionists may feel they are capable of playing a role in history other than that of victim. Killing tastes delicious when it is done for such an aim. "Either be a killer, or be the one killed" — this is the narrow choice they have set before themselves. In the court/stage the lawyer interrogates an Israeli soldier who took part in the massacre:

Lawyer: Is it true that you are working for this country, and that all your life you have felt that the Arabs are our enemies?

Soldier: Yes.

Lawyer: Is it true that you have these feelings against the Arabs in Israel, as well as the Arabs outside of it?

Soldier: Yes. I see no difference between them.

Lawyer: Is it true you felt that if you hadn't carried out the order to kill all Arabs in Kufr Qasem who were outside their homes, then you would have felt you had betrayed the spirit instilled in you in the Army and the Border Guard?

Soldier: Yes.

Lawyer: If, during the [1956] war, you were walking in a street in say, Jaffa, and you ran in to an Arab, would you have shot him?

Soldier: I don't know.

Judge: Suppose you had the following experience in Kufr Qasem. After 5 p.m. a woman calls out to you, and you are certain she is not dangerous and does not threaten the security of the state. She wants to ask a question, or ask for permission to pass to her house, and let us say that this takes place at 5:20. Supposing this woman was only ten meters

113

away from her house and she asked you for permission to go into it, what would you have done?

Soldier: I wouldn't have allowed her.

Judge: What would you have done?

Soldier: If she were in the street, I would've shot her.

Judge: But you were not in any danger. All that happened was that a certain person, because of a certain mistake, who did not know about the curfew order, came forward and asked for permission to cross the street, the question is then, would you still have killed everyone, or would you have refrained from killing in certain circumstances?

Soldier: I wouldn't have made any distinctions.

Judge: Would you have killed everyone?

Soldier: Yes.

Judge: Even if that person were a woman or a child?

Soldier: Yes.

Judge: You would have killed everyone you had seen?

Soldier: Yes.

And that was what actually took place.

The goat of Talal Shaker Issa, a child of eight, had run away from the courtyard into the street. Neither the child nor the goat understood that the curfew order had just gone into effect in the village a few hours before. The child ran after the goat, and the bullets fell upon him like rain and killed him.

His father followed, and the rifle carried on with its mission.

The wife ran toward her husband and her son, and the rifle continued with its mission. Their daughter, Noura, followed her parents and her brother, and the rifle still continued with its mission.

Now what was the mission of that rifle?

On the eve of the tripartite attack on Egypt in 1956, the brigade commander Colonel Shadmi called the battalion commander Major Malinki to his headquarters and gave him the orders for the unit under his command. The Border Guard was charged with the imposition of a total curfew that kept the villagers living in Kufr Qasem and the other villages in the Central Area restricted to their homes from five in the evening till six in the morning. The following exchange took place between the two commanders, which is now part of the District Court record:

Shadmi: The curfew must be absolute, and maintained with a strong arm, not just by arresting those who don't observe it, but by shooting them. It's better to kill them than have to deal with the complications that follow upon arrest.

Malinki: What will be the fate of citizens who know nothing about the curfew if they should run into the Border Guard on their way home from outside the village?

Shadmi: I don't want any sympathy. God have mercy on their souls!

At the end of this quick and decisive exchange, Malinki issued an order to the captain of the reserves attached to his platoon that contained the following:

"No dweller is permitted to be outside his house during the curfew. He who leaves his house is to be shot, and there will be no arrests."

The following exchange took place between Malinki and his soldiers, as can be determined from the records of the District Court:
Soldier: What shall we do with the wounded?

Malinki: There should be no concern with them. They must not be moved. There will be no wounded.

A platoon leader asked: What about women and children?

Malinki: No emotions!

Same platoon leader: What about those who are coming back from work?

Malinki: They get the same treatment as all the rest. These are the leader's orders. May God have mercy on their souls! . . .

So under his own authority and that of the government, forty-nine Arab citizens of the village of Kufr Qasem were shot down by the Border Guard. Among these were seven boys and girls and nine women.

Ten years after the massacre . . . Saleh Khalil Issa, who had miraculously escaped death, related to the poet Tawfiq Zayyad his eyewitness account:

In a while we heard shooting. I began to sense that danger was at hand and said to my cousin, "Let's go back," but he encouraged me to go on. There was a sheikh with us, around sixty years old, and he also encouraged us with verses from the Qur'an. We came closer until we were about one hundred meters from the nearest house in the village.

All of a sudden a man from the Border Guard appeared and blocked our way: "Halt!" Even till that moment I was expecting to be beaten, but not to be killed.

We got off our scooters, and the soldier ordered us to stand in line: "Where are you from?"
"From Kufr Qasem," we all said in one voice.

"Where were you?"
"At work."

He moved about five meters away, where there were two of his colleagues with machine guns, and shouted:

"Mow them down!"

I couldn't believe it was happening until I heard the bullets pouring in our direction. The first wave was at aimed our feet; the second a little higher. I fell to the ground with the others. Next to me was a horse cart whose owner they had detained and shot along with us. I fell behind the cart, I don't know how. I felt I was alive only after I had fallen. That is all. The three soldiers then moved till they were ten meters away.

In a few moments a truck arrived. They stopped it and ordered the people riding in the back to come down. There were many people (I later found out there were twenty-three) who were employees of the Osamia agricultural company.

The same soldier who gave the order to shoot us came forward and ordered them to come down and line up behind the vehicle. After they had lined up very close to each other, he moved away from them and shouted:

"Mow them down!"

A few got away but the majority fell. The three killers then came to where I was and the other scooter riders who were now dead and started to stack them into one pile three meters from where I was. They had heavy guns, and were finishing off the wounded.

They came near, and dragged the horse cart away. Its metal wheel with all its weight rolled over my foot. I clenched my teeth so as not to cry out. I pretended I was dead. They dragged me over to the pile and moved off.

Afterward they put those they had killed from the truck in a pile about ten meters away from us. Another truck arrived, with two people in it. They killed them. Then I heard the noise of a jeep coming down the road from the east, from the direction of the village. The motor was turned off, and I saw someone descending from it. I didn't understand what they were saying to each other, as they were about twenty meters away from me. Then the jeep went back in the direction it came from.

There was a period of quiet.

I saw the three killers walk away and sit at the edge of the village well. Then another truck came. (You might have noticed that they killed each group a few meters away from

117

the preceding group but in the opposite direction so that the new group would not be able to see what happened to the previous one.) But the vehicle I just mentioned passed right by the pile of dead bodies, and it seemed the killers no longer cared whether the new victims saw what happened to the previous ones or not. The vehicle passed to the side of the pile of bodies in the middle of which I was lying.

I heard women's voices. Later I found out there were thirteen women from the age of twelve up, and four men.

Suddenly, the three killers ran behind this car and stopped it. They ordered all the passengers out. I thought the car was between twenty and twenty-five meters away, and I felt an immense strength taking hold of me. I stood up and started running. I didn't know how I jumped a fence that was facing me there. Unconsciously, I ran in a direction parallel to the car. The bullets descended on me like a heavy rain. The sound of the bullets was mixed up with the wailing of the women and the sound of bodies falling to the ground. I felt a bullet penetrate my clothes. Only then did I realize where I was. I fell to the ground and started to crawl in the direction of an olive orchard. I imagined the orchard was full of army and military vehicles, and that I would run into them any moment. I hid behind a big rock under an olive tree, thinking of the death that might overtake me at any moment. I stayed there till morning, my hands and legs bleeding. Two soldiers discovered me, and I was taken to a hospital.

The next morning the criminals searched for a way to bury their crimes. They brought some people from the neighboring village of Jaljuliya to the Kufr Qasem graveyard and ordered them to dig forty-seven graves. Those charged with digging the graves did not know anything about the crime. They had only to dig . . .

. . . Kufr Qasem does not hold a significant place in the history of Palestine, and the poetic imagination cannot depict it in

118

glowing colors. But that setting sun, standing watch over the blood about to be shed, made of little-known Kufr Qasem the epic story of an enduring people. One evening, as we stood at the village gates, we felt the sharp pain of the joy pent up within us, and understood the crime for which we have been rewarded with all this punishment. We realized that stones are made of time, and we sat down on them to sing to the homeland.

Translated by Ibrahim Muhawi

Joy Ladin

A STRAND OF THICK BLACK HAIR

March 29, 2002

May Allah have mercy on you, oh Ayat Al-Akhras. You left your home for the path of martyrdom and Paradise . . . There was nothing to stop you.

— Dr. Khalil Ibrahim Al-Sa'adat, *Al-Jezirah* columnist

It was a typical Friday afternoon in the Kiryat Hayovel neighborhood of southern Jerusalem. At the Supersol market, the Sabbath rush was underway . . . When the smoke cleared and the screaming stopped, the two teenage girls and the guard lay dead, three more victims of the madness of martyrdom.

— Joshua Hammer, *Newsweek*

Establishment publications like . . . Newsweek *attempt to show their "compassion" and "even-handedness" by suggesting that all parties to the conflict are equally victims, and all are equally terrorists. In the process, they dishonor the dead by erasing the necessary dividing line between the blameless and the bestial. . . . These distinctions are essential in order to preserve clear thinking about the unfolding struggle in the Middle East.*

— Michael Medved, *WorldNetDaily*

May Allah have mercy on you
Oh Ayat Al-Akhras

And may that mercy comprehend
The security guard who blocks your path

The belt of explosives across your hips
Rachel Levy eager for fish

And the strand of thick black hair
Yours or Rachel's an essential distinction

Impossible to make
Now that the smoke has cleared

She could be your twin
Columnists insist, struck by the echo

Eerie they call it
Between AP photographs

Unfinished adolescent faces
Plucked brows pitched at improbable angles

Mercy can't comprehend
But you Jacob understand

The blessing that is this land
Rides on the resemblance

Between the hand of the hunter
The other the twin

And the skin of slaughtered kid
You wrap around your wrists

I smell your clothes
And the smell of your flesh

Is the smell of fields
The Lord has blessed

Abundance of grain and wine
Kine and kid

Are you really my son Esau
You say I am

Be master I say over your brothers
The smoke has cleared the screaming stopped

Go and buy some fish

•

Rachel is weeping for her children
Not a footfall in the street

Her blood's been swept
Flesh gathered sifted wrapped

But something of her persists
Enough to fall in love with

To refuse
To be comforted

The bodies were blown
In opposite directions

"Esau" and "Jacob" "victim" and "terrorist"
Her face remained intact
Lips full eyes a ewe's
Soft but confident

Nitza Agam

BLACKOUT

He threw an apple and a toothbrush
into his worn, brown duffel bag
from the back of the closet
along with his rifle.

He kissed me quickly,
I asked him if I could
walk him to the road.
He said "No."

I was left to board up our one room
cottage with black cloth
over the windows
Black cloth to hide behind
Black cloth to make believe
I was not there
I would not
I could not
be seen.

Later the soldiers
who had been with him in the tank
told me his lungs
like a thousand pieces of glass
Split.

His face and body
untouched
perfect
no sign of blood
clear blue eyes closed
just asleep.

His lungs
like the bombs that hit
that shatter glass
split into themselves.

At the temporary military cemetery,
his former girlfriend
beat me to his grave,
I was still
jealous of her beauty.

She flung herself on the grave
and wailed in rhythmic
ancient Hebrew fashion.

Did she love him more?
If I loved him as much,
Could I, too, keen?

I just stood there
watching.

The sound of crying
rose up like the black curtain
over my window
like the sirens that sounded
when the war broke out.
I tried to grieve
but did not know how
or for what.

Yousef el Qedra

ON THE MARGIN OF A WHIRLWIND

Resurrection is crawling . . .
The beginning is all about horses of cloud
circling God's sky over Gaza City.
These clouds descend on the ancient shores of the people
while a woman of a volcano erupts
in song on the waterline of the lazy blue beach.
Windmills of butterflies are making the whole world
dance to the dream lost behind dielectric walls.
The wind embraces twilight on an igniting sea.
My cytoplasms formed from blood and misbegotten
human beings are arrayed on a rose-colored glass plate.
She alone holds the book of love and combs the trees' hair.
Anxiety is sailing on the margin of a whirlwind
leading to a window inside the book.
The topic is war . . .

Resurrection is rising to its feet . . .
Horses of fire and steel kneaded the flesh of a youngster
    fleeing Gaza.
His terrified brother stole his broken arm and planted it
    under a tree,
whose tears bewail the destruction. This tree as the boy
    understands it
is a dedicated guard, whereas the cemetery is far away
and the hell you trust does not exclude making shrines.

Resurrection is scaling the ladders of dissonance,
enters the room of a young woman to burn an album;
the woman was hiding smiles for her children
who would emerge from hope and a love story
    never completed.
For fire broke out inside her lover's heart.

And he could not defeat two fires, so he surrendered to oblivion.
Except that he told how the fire coming from her window
merged with the fire coming from his balcony
where he was waiting for her.

January 29, 2009

Translated by Yasmin Snounu and Edward Morin

Ada Aharoni

THIS CURSED WAR

inspired by an Israeli Soldier's Yom Kippur War Diary,
October 1973

The night creeps along, funeral throng
darkens. Memories rush and flood blood.
Blossoming list of dead thumps red.
Every name pins mind with whizzing missiles,
  Cursed, cursed war!

In jeep on Golan Heights, loneliest I have ever been,
I watch skeletons of tanks, crowned with names of friends,
Sinister row, black graves, fresh bodies — old smell.
  Cursed, cursed war!

It doesn't look at all like wars in films this war,
Here we do not get a chance to shoot, or wave a flag,
Shrieking shells, hyena lightning pour on us, and we run
backwards or forwards or to the side,
And some are saved and some are not,
Not all, not always; but always cursing
  This cursed, cursed war!

In an English centurion holding Belgian guns,
We watch two American-made airplanes
Shot down by Russian-made missiles.
I cannot hate the Syrian on the other side
Who holds a French gun and shoots Soviet Sams;
We are toy soldiers of shopkeepers
Who want to sell — selling us, in this
  Cursed, cursed war!

God, let it stop, let it end,
Let the nightmare end!
Cursing is the only shelter
We can creep into, not to crumble
Before thoughts in the dark.
Cursed are those who force me to be here
      Cursed be this cursed, cursed war!

Fadwa Tuqan

MY SAD CITY

(The Day of Zionist Occupation)

The day we saw death and betrayal,
The tide ebbed,
The windows of the sky closed,
And the city held its breath.
The day the waves were vanquished, the day
The ugliness of the abyss revealed its true face,
Hope turned to ashes,
And gaging on disaster,
My sad city choked.

Gone were the children and the songs,
There was no shadow, no echo.
Sorrow crawled naked in my city,
With bloodied footsteps.
Silence reigned in my city,
Silence heavy like crouching mountains,
Mysterious like the night, tragic silence,
Burdened,
Weighed down with death and defeat.
Alas! My sad and silent city:
Can it be true that in the season of harvest,
Grain and fruit have turned to ashes?
Alas! That this should be the fruit of all the journeying!

Translated by A.M. Elmesseri

Marjorie Stamm Rosenfeld

TZAMA

Beneath the Holy Land,
where even water wars are fought,
the troubled springs run deep.
And water, which has properties
to wear on stone, has split the rock.
Lord . . .
                    my shepherd.

About suffering, Stefan Grass said,
"Suffering is like salt, bitter in a glass.
Become a lake instead—then sip the water.
You'll see how sweet it tastes,
with hardly any hint of bitterness."

(The Jaffa oranges are sweet
and bigger than grenades.
We've moved our fences farther in.
Our neighbors claim the land we left,
then ours.)

                    Beside the still waters . . .
Sbarro Pizza,
where a young man opens up his coat,
says to the girl behind the counter,
Know what this is?
so like the exhibitionist
who bares his misused, misplaced
instrument of love
explosively.
                    He maketh me to lie down . . .

In green pastures
tents of Palestinians
are buffeted by angry winds,
their throats are parched.
The houses of the Palestinians collapse.

In the house of the Lord,
another scene: From one side
comes a swarthy man and from the other,
one more swarthy man —
sons of the same father.
They face off, raise their instruments,
and aim. Which will give ground?
Which strike the other first?
Raging thirst propels them.
Nearby the only lake
that's fresh and clear
is Lake Tiberius,
called the Sea of Galilee.
It, too, is troubled water.
Further south, the sea is dead
and full of salt. How many more
Abramic sons must fall?

(Bombs bloom.
The wolves that used to roam
the Russian Steppes
are here.)

Through the valley of the shadow,
a great tree arches over the River Jordan.
It is the tree of the Jewish people.
It is the tree of the Palestinian people.
Its leaves shudder in the wind,
on every leaf a name.

Tzama is the Hebrew word for "thirst."

Samih al-Qasim

LETTER FROM A PRISON CAMP

Mother, it grieves me
That because of me, throughout your night of agony,
You shed silent tears, anxiously awaiting the return
Of my beloved brothers from their chores;
That you are not able to eat
While my seat remains empty, and there is no talk or laughter.
How it pains me, Mother,
That tears rush to your eyes
When friends drop by to ask about me.
But I believe, Mother,
That the splendor of life
Is being born within the walls of my prison,
And I believe that the last of my visitors
Will not be an eyeless bat, coming to me by night.
Surely, the light of day will dawn,
And, dazzled by it, my jailer will be humbled.
He will fall to the ground . . . broken,
Shattered, burnt by daylight.

Translated by A.M. Elmesseri

Adam Schonbrun

CHANA OF THE AGES

I'm speaking of the poet
Who dreamed her son died
In Lebanon — the words
She wrote to him, the loss
She felt before he'd gone.

Horror, to see so far, so much
Yet, could she change anything?
Her son went off. She kept
Her harried mother's heart
Close over him.

The boy knew his mother was right.
He lay there atop his duffel bag,
Empty, looking at the sky, Phantoms,
F-16's, the heat blurring, this war
He hated finally left him.

In the Shuf Mountains, he bled to death.
His mother's poems in his fatigues.

Mike Maggio

DIRGE

once we could look at the sky—
birds would flutter from roof to bough
their tiny voices the clicking of cool pearls
plush clouds would roll by
on ambling afternoons
sometimes
like floats on parade
and when we least expected
the rain would come
a sudden celebration
a swell of slick black nylon
dripping plump silver raindrops
like joyful tears
when the bride and groom first kissed
amid a shower of white rice and cascading confetti—

once we could look at the cool blue sky

•

The best measure
is to have the proper protective clothing
and gas mask.
If these are not available
you should move as quickly as possible
into a building.
Seal windows and doors
reduce ventilation, turn off A/C.
Stay in the room with the lowest air flow.
Breath through a dense towel
or better yet
use towel wrapped around a dry piece of charcoal.

Impervious clothing
such as raincoat and tight goggles
can help.
Head and body hair should be covered.
DO NOT leave the building
or open any doors to the outside.
Chemicals should disperse in one to two hours.

After the chemicals have dissipated
quickly leave the area of contamination.
DO NOT pick up items from the outside.

•

I remember the Kurds—
there's a picture in *Time* magazine
faces frozen
like porcelain dolls
carelessly laid
unknown, forgotten folk
sleeping now
peacefully at last

what had they done to deserve such immortality

their villages I hear were once filled with song—
the flute and the tambourine
children dancing at the wedding celebration
clean bright costumes whirling
around their unsuspecting lives

do you remember the Kurds
their national song silenced
cottages flattened
bodies strewn like matchsticks along the roadside
that strange imposed sleep

all that's left

•

One day the soldiers came.
It was *fajr*
or just before
so much has happened I can't remember.
But what we heard was not the *azzan*
         what we saw was not the sunrise

(birds dropping from trees
yellow clouds blistering in the sky
cats, dogs, people choking
where do I run
where are the children)

When the shooting was over
when the radio station went off the air
when days maybe weeks had passed
and our food supplies ran thin
we got in our cars
shot straight for the desert.

An old Bedouin guided us to the border.
He knew every dune, every *wadi*
like the wife he had loved since his sixteenth year.

It was his way of serving, he said.
Would do so till they shot him.

May God protect his gentle soul.

•

we sit and wait

    (will the sun rise tomorrow
     will the birds sing their song)

despair, hope, wonder

(so many stories to be told
so many yet to be born
so many never to be known)

will anyone hear
will anyone ever really hear

Molly Spencer

CEASE-FIRE

Israel suspended its military operations in Gaza
for three hours on Wednesday to allow humanitarian aid
and fuel for power generation to reach Gazans,
who used the afternoon break to shop.

— *The New York Times,* 7 January 2009

Three hours
they have set aside,
not for peace, but a promise
not to kill my child your child
on our doorsteps. Now
we go out into wide-open
sunlight. My hands your hands,
they seek the same treasures:
little food, little water, slice
of sky, sip of fresh air. Time
to wash and cover our dead,
pull them to the graves. A face
to see my face, to say again
how swiftly life ends
in one home, goes on
same as yesterday next door.
Three hours they keep the promise
to rest heavy arms
while we water the seeds
of mere life, another day turning
toward night. Here,
through this window this doorway
this three-hour promise,
I see you see me. I see you
see me.

Helen Bar-Lev

AN OCTOBER THURSDAY MORNING

We should have been tired last night
but weren't
were not in bed at midnight
yet chose not to hear the news

Now it is early morning Thursday
sleep has been short and dreamless
the pillow does not give as much comfort
after an attack and the body aches
with the strain of waiting;
only the ears are not exhausted

We have a cousin in that city
who was at the market a few hours
before the attack
and heard the explosion from her flat

And of course you used to go there often
when you lived in the adjacent town

They were all our ages, the five who died
beyond their prime
and having contributed already to society,
this is no tremendous tragedy,
and the country sighs with collective relief
that the children were all in school

One of the dead was Arab, why not?
One has the same last name as our neighbors upstairs.
is that why they were so quiet last night?

Thursday morning
hugs are suspended
the telephone rings
it is the man from the internet provider
to address a question

Business as usual
and five more funerals

Adam Schonbrun

MESSIANIC HOT PEPPER POEM

(details from South Lebanon)

When the army laid out
The bodies of the four
Party-of-God Terrorists
I noticed lying next to
The silencer & Kalashnikovs
A bottle of Harissa hot sauce
& wondered what they ate
before they were shot &
remembered my New Orleans Jazz
Hope that cayenne could unite the world
Not in violence but
In one peaceful feast
One communal shindig,
A messianic rush
Where even the dead get their hearts beating
To the peppers that make us sigh
For water & prayer.

Sam Hamod

SABRA/SHATILLA: IN SORROW

It is nothing, the blood
red   into stony ground,   nothing,   we can say
nothing, the flares red and white, blue, nothing
against black sky, faces blur, nothing
sharp rope cuts into wrists, it is
nothing, slash of knife on throat, gurgling, knowing
nothing, phalangist, israeli, we hear phalange not
spoken, it is in the face, *frangiiyah'*, *gemeyal*, it is
nothing, mustache moves,
nothing, these words
nothing, *thunk, thunk* of bazookas,   crunch
of bone, nothing, it is nothing, the
children run hiding under the bed
like play, a man comes in
they say nothing, he laughs, tells them
they'll be safe, nothing, no sound, he
shouts, "Come out!" nothing
he lifts the bed,
their big eyes open,
he laughs,
his Uzi sputters —
they are nothing
their flesh nothing
oh, it is nothing
do not worry, they are
nothing, it is
nothing, do not worry, nothing
has happened,
nothing, it is nothing, say it is nothing —

so be peaceful brothers and sisters   do not run away
we are all Arabs   we will do nothing   it is nothing
we do nothing   it is nothing   it didn't happen   if it did
it is nothing   oh, it is nothing
nothing at all
and now say it and believe it, it is nothing
nothing   nothing
oh God   nothing.

Ada Aharoni

REMEMBER ME EVERY TIME
THE MOON RISES OVER THE SPHINX

*inspired by an Egyptian soldier's diary
found in the Sinai, after the Yom Kippur War, October 1973*

Dear Leila, to you my love
I breathe my last letter.
I love you in all the ways love means —

Remember me every time the sun sets over the Pyramids
and the moon rises over the Sphinx

Today marks the ninth year
of my enrolling at the cursed military college.
If I knew then to what bitter thorns it would lead me —
the college would have never seen my face.
I loathe the hours a man goes through while waiting for death.

Remember me every time the sun sets over the Pyramids
and the moon rises over the Sphinx

I really believed what we were told,
that we, would never begin a war —
but we have been ordered to cross the Suez Canal,
and my blood, my bones know I have a few more hours to live.

I will fight and die for Allah and Egypt —
when what I want is to live
for you, my Leila,
loving you all my life,
        my Leila, my life.

Joy Ladin

THE SITUATION:
AN EXCLUSIVE SIMULCAST

•

Not long after the collapse of the Camp David peace talks, the Oslo peace accords—violated incessantly by both sides since their inception—were ritually slaughtered when soon-to-be Prime Minister Ariel Sharon, considered a war criminal by Palestinians, was permitted by the Israeli government to visit the site of the Second Temple where the Al-Aqsa Mosque is now located. Sharon's visit provided the pretext for a long-prepared resumption of the Palestinian intifada, armed rebellion against Israeli occupation. As months of intifada became years, Israelis and Palestinians fell into a bitter rhythm of suicide bombings and military retaliations, targeted assassinations and drive-by snipings, each side vying to move ahead in the body count while disclaiming all responsibility for the conflict.

There's no word for this self-perpetuating slaughter. Israelis call it *ha-Matzav,* "the Situation."

•

I'm sick of the Situation
That's what everyone says
I'm sick I'm everyone who says
The end has come all hope has fled
I'm the Situation

At first you watched me on television

I was this one's infant that one's limbs
A Jew-only road where security slipped
Pregnant, Palestinian

145

Now I'm a question

Of self-definition

Close as your mother's clippers
Working across your hands
Don't move she says and you won't get hurt
Holds you still — diminishes —

Wraps you Jacob may I call you Jacob

In swathes of slaughtered kid
To steal the blessing
You claim by right
I'm with you 100%

I'm the market you're afraid to shop in

The women who urge you to squeeze their fruits
The embarrassing non-lethal object
The guard pulls out of your bag
Your sons and daughters

And enemies who look just like them
A vast miscellaneous throng
Trapped in a single skin
I'm Jacob's voice I'm Esau's hands
Or is that you

Burying yourself in him
No matter
You come with weeping and graciously I guide you
Explode your hopes
Reflect like a bathroom mirror
The drops that run

Between occupation and terror

Disappointments hopeless yearnings
For a swimming pool what's wrong with that
For cities you didn't build olives you didn't plant

For the twin

Who craves what you crave
Who lived where you live
To admit
He never existed

I cry out in joy for Jacob

Vineyard dangling
At the crossroads of the nations
My soul fails with longing
When I see you ripening there

Give me to eat of your red red stuff

I'm your father yes
The blood of Jacob is my meat
Esau—
Which son are you—
Esau is my bread

Judy Kronenfeld

CLEAN

Crime Scene Cleaners, Inc.
Homicide
Suicide
Accidental death
—*written on the side of a truck seen on the freeway*

Let them come like priests in white robes
and tenderly cleanse
the buttocks of the four-year-old
who shat in his pants, pressing his ears
against the scream of F16s
flying low over Gaza

Order them up for the smashed skull
at Haditha, the intestines' spill
out of back wounds, the graffiti-scrawled
house where "democracy
assassinated a family"

Let them restore
the "accidentally" killed
children fleeing on the road
from Marwaheen, obeying
blasting loudspeakers into
their deaths

Order them up for the spattered mall,
the hall, the checkpoint, the crossing,
the wall

Order them up for the broken-necked
girlfriend, left to drown in their tub
by the returning Marine
Order them up
for his crazed pain

Order them up for the port-a-potty
splattered with blood—
any soldier's whose wife's "bad news"
is the last strain

Let them "with utmost respect" take down
the three "smart," "creative," "committed"
prisoners who hanged themselves
with bedsheets and clothes in Guantanamo,
their act "not desperation"
but "warfare waged against us"

Let them remove the bindings
around the necks, the plastic bags
over the heads, let them
wash out the shot-through mouths
of men revenged, let them re-leaf
the golden dome

Let the war presidents and prime
ministers and militia leaders,
for whom war is holy
or righteous, abstract,
mathematical, even joyous,
somehow made clean
in the mind,
be each given one small toothbrush,
and the sentence:
scour this blood

IV

Samih al-Qasim

A HOMELAND

So what,
When in my homeland
The sparrow dies of starvation,
In exile, without a shroud,
While the earthworm is satiated,
Devouring God's food!

So what,
When the yellow fields
Yield no more to their tillers
Than memories of weariness,
While their rich harvest pours
Into the granaries of the usurper!

So what,
If the cement has diverted
The ancient springs,
Causing them to forget their natural course,
When their owner calls,
They cry in his face: "Who are you?"

So what,
When the almond and the olive have turned to timber
Adorning tavern doorways,
And monuments
Whose nude loveliness beautifies halls and bars,
And is carried by tourists
To the farthest corners of the earth,
While nothing remains before my eyes
But dry leaves and tinder!

So what,
When my people's tragedy
Has turned to farce in others' eyes,
And my face is a poor bargain
That even the slave-trader gleefully distains!

So what,
When in barren space the satellites spin,
And in the streets walks a beggar, holding a hat,
And the song of autumn is heard!

Blow, East winds!
Our roots are still alive!

Mahmoud Darwish

Excerpt (3): JOURNAL OF AN ORDINARY GRIEF

— What are you doing, father?

— I'm searching for my heart, which fell away that night.

— Do you think you'll find it here?

— Where else am I going to find it? I bend to the ground and pick it up piece by piece just as the women of the fellahin pick up olives in October, one olive at a time.

— But you're picking up pebbles!

— Doing that is a good exercise for memory and perception. Who knows? Maybe these pebbles are petrified pieces of my heart. And even if they're not, I would still have gotten used to the effort of searching on my own for something that made me feel lost when it was lost. The mere act of searching is proof that I refuse to get lost in my loss. The other side of this effort is the proof that I am in fact lost as long as I have not found what I have lost.

— What else are you doing, father?

— When I chance upon pebbles that look like my heart, I transform them with my fingers on fire into words that put me in touch with the distant homeland. We then become a language that can turn into flesh.

— Is there something else you want to say?

— I do, but I don't understand the words, for the woman I'm talking to turns into another exile.

— When you were young, were you afraid of the moon?

— That's what they say. But it's not true that children are always afraid of the moon.

If it weren't for the moon, I would've become an orphan before my time. It hadn't yet fallen into the well. It was higher than my forehead and closer than the mulberry tree in the middle of my grandfather's yard. The dog used to bark when the full moon rose. When the first shots rang out, I was surprised that a wedding celebration should be taking place that evening. And when they led me away to join the long caravan, the moon was our companion on a road that later I understood was the road of exile.

Translated by Ibrahim Muhawi

Marjorie Stamm Rosenfeld

HERE-THERE SPRING

for the citizens of Sderot

Here, where the sky
has stitched two clouds together,
two brown doves have been sitting
on the wall outside my kitchen window,
their heads at forty-five degrees
of separation, tails crossed in an X
which cancels something out.

Do you remember how hopeful
you once were each spring—the world
newly formed and all of it in flower?
Now a fractured sky. Red dawn.
The shriek of rockets.

Peach trees have donned white robes.
Acacias have put on their crowns.
On your sill, Cousin, a white butterfly
puts down, a piece of pale lace fluttering,
impervious to distance. Even in the desert
there are these butterflies. The whole
world hatches out, sky cerulean,
just as the world,
sprung into blossom,
breaks.

Khaled Abdallah

EXCHANGE

I slept like the dead in the palm of the funeral. And when
    I woke
my hand found two gloves made of dough resting on my heart.
    I remembered
that our hands in the world were cold like two fish swimming
in the air. And two branches of no
import to prophets who practice carpentry. I slept
in the palm that forgets to open up in the morning. And I forgot
that I was supposed to wake.

EMPTY

Whenever they hooded his eyes in hide and go seek
he forgot them because they shut him out.
He became a cloud that found its rain.
And on his way to earth it took him
and led him to a distant country
and scattered him as snow on the shadow of a woman
    waiting for a train.
He thrashes at space like a cat that children have placed
    in a plastic bag.
Who will send a hook and pole to fish his soul from
    under the water?
He knows this density. If he could cleave it
he would breathe deeply and die.

Translated by Khaled Mattawa

158

Seema V. Atalla

COLD COMFORT

The lost places are easy to list:

My grandmother's Haifa
where she wore her hair in waist-long braids,
gathered with her neighbors by the seaside to chat,
and ate the tiny, crisp fish she loved, fried to perfection.

My father's Nazareth
where he carried grain to the mill for his mother,
and listened to the blind man who sat outside the church
playing hymns on his flute.

My grandmother's Jerusalem
where she planted banks of fragrant lavender,
taught kindergarten,
and rolled grape leaves for dinner, leaf by leaf.

My mother's Ramallah
cool green peaceful place
where she and her sisters learned algebra and embroidery
among the sighing pines and rosy stone homes.

Those places are unrecognizable now
disfigured
by misery
riddled with desperation
choked with the nitty gritty grime of actuality.

Simpler to turn back to the long-cherished images.
The lost places seem quaint now,
perhaps a little faded . . .
we revisit them

the way we touch an old injury,
fingering the scar
over and over
finding comfort
in pressing the place
where it hurts.

Naomi Shihab Nye

HOW PALESTINIANS KEEP WARM

Choose one word and say it over
and over, till it builds a fire inside your mouth.
Adhafera, the one who holds out, *Alphard,* solitary one,
the stars were named by people like us.
Each night they line up on the long path between worlds.
They nod and blink, no right or wrong
in their yellow eyes. *Dirah,* little house,
unfold your walls and take us in.

My well went dry, my grandfather's grapes
have stopped singing. I stir the coals,
my babies cry. How will I teach them
they belong to the stars?
They build forts of white stone and say, "This is mine."
How will I teach them to love *Mizar,* veil cloak,
to know that behind it an ancient man
is fanning a flame?
He stirs the dark wind of our breath.
He says the veil will rise
till they see us shining, spreading like embers
on the blessed hills.

Well, I made that up. I'm not so sure about *Mizar.*
But I know we need to keep warm here on earth
and when your shawl is as thin as mine is, you tell stories.

Adhafera: The University of Illinois astronomy department
explains this word as "the lock of hair." In this case, the lock of
hair not combed in smoothly.

Dafna Hornike

BITTER ALMONDS

In this landscape of
home the
walls grow like rows of almond trees
that used to belong to someone.
Lines of deserted curved symbols,
carving the Judea mountains,
now they are unwanted, bitter.

I go further away,
away from this divided home,
into cultivated orchards,
still searching for walls, fences, bricks,
something to orient myself with
in all this darkness.

I'll miss you I said
to my unwanted home
and really meant to say
I need to get away from
all these walls.

Yousef el Qedra

EXHAUSTION OVERTOOK ME

June 14, 2009

I've suffered from fatigue since an early age.
And my body crumpled in the presence of sickness.
Probably, my body also fell apart.
No longer am I some firm-rooted tree,
branches mingling with the clear blue sky.
Maybe I have never been that way.
Every cell in my body was shaken.
You saw so many thorny questions grown into my skin.
You saw that my eyes hurt with tears,
and I couldn't tell from which cascade those tears fell.

You saw clouds that appeared in the minds of my poems
heading back in disappointment toward the river;
the river reverted to its headwaters of first longing.
The sea is too salty. Meanwhile, my thirst surprised me
by coming at the wrong time. My thirst was stubborn,
and I am not stubborn with anyone, except myself.

Suddenly, I wanted the world to turn into a desert
without a sun above it. Without memories of the trees
or the river or the distraught young women.
I want myself to be a dead body
smoking a rotten cigarette, watching the emptiness.
I want myself to be a line inside a neglected book,
a line upon which the dust eats and drinks.

Translated by Yasmin Snounu and Edward Morin

Tom Berman

GREENING DAYS

after the rains
come
the greening days

untaught seedlings
harboring
no memories
of summer drought
or arid autumn
seek
an insentient
cerulean sky

when new hope
is a rare commodity
there's true joy
in the unfurling
of a leaf
and the trusting growth
of newborn grass

Khaled Abdallah

SLUMBER

A rat skitters toward a cardboard box. The dirty toddler climbs
the ladder holding the wash line. The neighborhood women
   chew on a plant
that resembles your inner voice. And I (bothered thus) hear
only what I wish. My lap is brimful
of your elevated songs. The toddler comes down safely.
   And we all sleep.
When my brother wakes me I return from a spot where I was
   drinking
something with you, something like iced coffee. There are
   rocks and moss and water
and much air and wind and snow and violins straining
   and taut and books, and day-old food
and a hair clip, and a single hair long and stretched like
   hibernation,
and that's why I seem like a scowling monkey when I wake.

Translated by Khaled Mattawa

Khaled Abdallah

MINT

I walk barefoot into my mother's talk,
the dusty square, the garden chair, the dancer's kerchief, the wind,
eyes from windows opposite, a moon dangled between two palm
    fronds and another moon at the window.
The dancer has a bird's fluttering heart that no chest can contain.
A jug sprinkles water to settle the dust.
The flute's lip is wet with its player's saliva. Like children's saliva
on the throat of a balloon. This tune: your heart's demons
    will keep it
like the color of your first school uniform. But if the accordion
    went mad
the women who believe in luck will say this boy is jinxed.
They would prepare a necklace for him made of two threads from
    the sacks
of relief flour and the bones of extinct animals and shells and yellow
fangs. I return barefoot to mother's talk. "Another moon at the
window."
"Build some corners in your heart, my love, and hide your mint
    plants among them."

Translated by Khaled Mattawa

Seema V. Atalla

VISITING THE WEST BANK

Once a year up the long road from Jericho. Hot summer.

Mothballs in knots of tulle, lavender sachets.
Suitcases dragged down from the attic, their locks sprung open
elaborate embroidery explained, unfolded
beautiful handknit sweaters for trying on.

Every time we arrived, this unloading began—
from freezer and pantry the delicacies of each season
vine leaves wrapped in April
winter's marmalade, quince jelly
zaatar dried in June.

As though life when we left stopped passing
started piling up
packing itself neatly into shoebox and suitcase
preserving itself in the pantry with pickles and jam.

Even the gossip postponed
each anecdote sealed away
saved to be savored
at this annual sharing.

Daily, at the windowsill, chickenwire. Loudspeakers.

In each suitcase a sachet of sorrow never unpacked.

Naomi Shihab Nye

MY FATHER, ON DIALYSIS

wrote a book about Palestine called
DOES THE LAND REMEMBER ME?

He wrote it in longhand on scraps of paper
as his blood filtered through the big machine

He was not afraid to watch it
circulate

Nurses and aides asked him
What are you doing?

He said, Planting a garden
Of almonds and figs

Dipping sprigs of mint into
glasses of steaming tea

breathing the damp stones
of my old city

pressing my mind into the soul
of an olive tree

Mahmoud Darwish

CONCERNING HOPES

Tell me not:
     I wish I were a baker in Algeria
     That I might sing with a freedom fighter.
Tell me not:
     I wish I were a shepherd in Yemen
     That I might sing of the eruptions of time.
Tell me not:
     I wish I were a waiter in Havana
     That I might sing of the victories of the sorrowful.
Tell me not:
     I wish I were a young porter in Aswan
     That I might sing to the rocks.

My friend!
The Nile will never flow into the Volga,
Nor will the Congo or the Jordan River flow into the Euphrates.
Each river has its own source, its course, and its life.
My friend! Our land is no barren land.
Each land is born in due time;
With every dawn, a freedom fighter rises.

Translated by A. M. Elmesseri

169

Sami Al Jundi

TAKE ME TO AL-QASTAL

There, in the cradle of yearning
Where the birds circle in cheerless skies
In the pine forests,
There rest the souls of the ancients
Did you ask the Swallow, my friend,
About Al-Qastal?

From a hill looking over Deir Yassin
Where love was first born
Thousands of years ago
Before the birth of Christ
Before the budding of jasmine
By the cradle of the goldfinch
Be sure to ask about Al-Qastal.

A deep valley
A mystifying magic and nectar of secrets
A flock of pigeons and a nightingale
And the remains of a forgotten village and a cross
Ruins of a Babylonian minaret
There, where the moon is near
And our first concern is
Love and Al-Qastal.

Take me to Al-Qastal
Take me to the beautiful grave
Take me to my last home
And load me up with the tragedies of the Arabs
And all the fragrance of the ancestors

My home is the prettiest
My grave is the largest
My path is to Al-Qastal.

Translated by Amal Eqeiq

KNOWING

On April 16, 1953, Eleanor Roosevelt wrote a letter
to my father answering one of his own.
No, she said. I do not think Arab refugees
should be permitted to return to their homes
in Israel. There are few homes to return to.
His face, perfect burn of indignation.
He would carry his stolen home
into the next millennium and never enter it
again though it remains intact till now.
She numbered her answers.
2. I do not know if it is advisable
to internationalize Jerusalem.
She had worked for black youth, the unemployed.
She helped to found the United Nations.
She stood up for Marian Anderson when they wouldn't
let her sing. My dad, at 25, trying to support a wife
and baby in a tired American city, dreamed
his own place international so he might be included again.
He wanted to sing. In 2010 the same questions
dangle in air.
3. I do not know if there should be an Arab Palestine
as an independent state side by side with Israel.
Very sincerely yours. She signed the letter
with a shaky hand from her perch at Val-Kill Cottage, Hyde Park,
Dutchess County, New York. Such a nice address, unencumbered
by numbers or thieves. Eleanor did not know. She was honest
about not knowing. She would die
at 78 from bone marrow tuberculosis. He would die at 80
still frustrated, still writing letters. We live on, puzzles of power
unraveling around us, building new walls, proclaiming,
protesting. One phrase worth clinging to—side by side.
My mother says, he wrote her often.
This was not her only reply.

J. Weintraub

TO THE DIAMOND PEDDLER STEINBERG/POSTMARK: BEIRUT/ NO RETURN ADDRESS/1979

Lemony tea and crumpets mingled among
mail fluttering like doves. Secretaries waved
good morning and Reuters stuck out its tongue.

"Bank on these," he recalled having told his son—
as he watched the stones of his scimitar shine,
as the envelope sizzled beneath the blade—
"as sure as Rolls Royce or a ten percent note
with the Bank of England. Milled in mother earth's rind.
The reichsmark may fall and the pound may float,
the price of the dollar will always vary,
but a diamond is forever, as long as the sale
is policed and men and women still marry."

And were these his thoughts as he opened his mail
and watched his hand torn asunder,
his flesh leap from his bones?
Or did he indeed wonder
that he could so easily soar—
be at one with history,
with God's chosen, alone
with the sons of Galilee's

salty shore?

Marian Haddad

THE MAP ON MY FRIEND'S WALL

for Naomi Shihab Nye

Granddaughter
of Sitti Khadra,
I did not know you
until I picked
your book off a shelf
over fifteen years ago.

It's there I read
about your yellow glove,
a red suitcase, your Uncle
Mohammad and the broom-
maker in Palestine,
the way you made it seem
he was a master
of this one lost art,

how he woke up
and began to weave
the seam around the straw,
stitched it into place,
taking such care,
as if it were something
his own wife would wear.

The way I saw your name
and it rang clear,
something in it meant
you were quite like me.

A name – how we relate
to people from our lands,

though I still
have mine, but you
do not
have yours.
Syria is still
on the map,
and suddenly
it resonated loud
and clear, your Palestine
has been
erased
from the map
on my friend's
wall.

For some reason, it was then,
I began to study
where every country lay,
and something in me sought
the places of my race,

and I began to see
the space between
Syria and Lebanon,
and how it was O.K. —
the separate countries
that they made,
allowed the other
to exist;

I looked for Jordan,
Yemen, The United
Arab Emirates.
Morocco and El Jazayer,
Berber countries first,
how they embraced
the same language

our grandfathers
spoke, but they, still
able to keep
their own identities.

I saw Israel
and thought,
*Our neighbors, a part of us,
our space. A cup of sugar, please.*

And for a moment I forgot
a strange happening. I began to look
and look for one
country
I once had to name
on an old map.

My eye began to scan
the crevices in-between,
and a panic began
to stir somehow
inside the brain.

Unable to find
this one lost patch
of land, what color
was it then?

Oh, yes. I cannot even place
my finger atop
it's geographical brow,
the hump it might have made
under a braille hand
on the raised surface
of a sky blue globe.

It then made strange sense
to me, why I couldn't find it
between its cluster
of neighboring spots.

I was appalled to think
someone had buried it
while I wasn't looking
straight, and that I didn't go
to this one funeral
they must have had
somewhere
to mourn their dead.

We hear so often
on the news, a story
somehow far away,
and we
forget to place
this one reality
in our own
dark book,
until something wakes us
into shock, and me pointing
my fleshy finger
on a land I once knew
existed there, cancelled
out. What about Sandy,
and Paul, my brother's friend,
his father's father came
from there, her grandfather left it
for L.A., and now,
there is no finding it
again. The place from which
they stemmed

has blown up, city
of smoke, and the houses
they once villaged in,
playing the *nai* and the *durbuk*
villages where weddings took,
and church bells rang,
or the call to prayer
in a mosque,

the children
playing with sticks
in thin alleys
between houses,
the women
baking the *sej*
and picking mint
out of
their own
small yards.

Philip Metres

3 poems from
ALONG THE SHRAPNEL EDGE OF MAPS

for Huwaida Arraf

she inserts the inked ribbon of herself
against the black roller of history / a face to face

metal alphabetic legs of that inverted insect—
the rifles / that thrash the air as targets

scatter / she can't help / herself / something in her
is growing each time she turns into the rifle's

eye / is growing as she places herself in its loathing
its permanent erection / the helmeted conductor

batons his order / & the waltz begins / & she
follows the lead of inevitable lead / itching

to fly from its nested chamber / she is the bullet
unfired / the puppet who's unhitched

the strings / in the bullet on the bleached page
of this land / she rises into the light—

for Ezra Nawi

for Ezra would dive beneath the wall of the half-
demolished shell of a house / as if to stave off

the final destruction / ghost of where & what
he is / Jew & Arab / standing among Arabs who can't

understand why their house could not stand
& why the bulldozer's teeth must seethe into its chest

182

like a lung collapsing / on the video you hear
Ezra's adrenaline gasping / the shaking of his hands

the soldier binds in plastic cuffs tighter & then
tighter again / "why are you tightening them?"

the soldiers laugh / "is it funny, the kids will sleep outside?"
& "the only thing left here is hatred"

"I did what my heart told me to do" / he will lodge
an immediate appeal / for Ezra in Hebrew means "help"

Rabbi Erik (Arik) Asherman

The midrash says, when Hagar and Ishmael were banished
into the desert, before God builds a well, the angels

say, — What are you doing? Don't you know the *tsuris*
the Jewish people are going to suffer at the hands

of the children of Ishmael? & God, according to this midrash,
says, — right now, in front of me, there's a child. Right now

this child is innocent. When I call on them, the parents waken
their children to introduce them to us. Our nation lives in a bubble

in which it claims every action is carried out according to law.
But I hold in my heart the looks of children who return home

to see their house destroyed, a book piercing through the rubble,
families sitting on packed suitcases, the words

of a Palestinian boy they'd tied to a windshield that I'd freed —
who said that a tall man in a kippa came to his aid.

Bonnie J. Morris

A POETRY SLAM WITH GOD

God up there in her underwear
Slammed down her glass, shook her angry ass
And said, *Bad shit has come to pass.*

Jerusalem's red from the bleeding head
Of a running child. It drives Her wild.
She says to me, *Hypocrisy.*

How can you sleep, the dreams you keep
Where once that land was soft with sheep:
Now there's no fleece, no sister peace
Each angry nation pours libation,
Sends an all-male delegation.

God up there yells, *Tell me, Bon,*
What tab of Ecstasy were you on
When you lived there, at age twenty
In that Israel of plenty
Made love with a Jewish girl
Lived with her and touched her pearl
And thought you were so radical,
That junior year sabbatical

God says, so: you were a dyke.
Mazel tov! That's what I like.
But who stood on some West Bank ridge
Protecting all your privilege
Any time you felt the call
To go pray at the Wailing Wall?
Guys with guns; Israeli sons
And daughters. Sore of war to core.

God says, *Bon, when you were young*
Did you ever wrap your tongue
Around a nice Ramallah girl?
Now, THAT is rad. And, wow, too bad
You never walked into the road
Of Arab women's lovercode.

I'm twice as old as I was when
I thought I knew it all, back then
And will I see that place again?
Bon, everything you thought you were
Is not enough to honor Her.

Samuel Hazo

MEDITERRANEAN UPDATE

Whatever let it be a pleasure
    made it end like anything
    that dies before we think
    it should.
                The aisles of lavender,
    the sea "between the land,"
    the houses cut from rock
    where Yeats lived last, the yachts
    moored hull to hull at anchor,
    and the wind from Africa that's known
    as the *libeccio* are blurred
    like painter's pigments fractioned
    into bits.
                "Everything's the same
    but us," I said, "because
    we've come back once too often."
French television flashed
    a raid by F-16's in Gaza
    followed by a sacrificial bombing
    in Jerusalem.
                The detonated bodies
    sprawled alike.
                "Same intent,"
    I said, "but different weapons."
The prospect made me kick
    aside a core of cardboard
    from a toilet paper roll
    discarded near a dumpster.
                Later
    we paganized ourselves in sun
    and surf—our way of fiddling
    while tomorrow burned.

                            Romeos
    roamed the beach, sporting
    their scrotal pouches.
                        Women
    wore nil but thongs and pubic
    patches.
                So many thronged
    the waves I thought of mullets
    or alewives surging in frenzy . . .
Three hours east by air,
    oppressor and oppressed were being
    filmed in battles we would watch
    while dining later in Antibes
    or sipping cappuccino by the pool.

Dana Negev

SHAME

Today I saw
A bumper sticker at the market
It said . . . *Shame on Israel* . . .
Just like that
On a blue truck in front of me
And for a moment I thought
Did they mean
Shame on me?

But, turning on my ignition
I said, in fact I understand,
And agree
Only I wasn't sure about
the word shame
on a blue truck
Just like that.

So I drove along
In my black Subaru
Protected from the cold and dust
My windows rolled up high
Protected from the homeless
(I hear in Brazil
They can rob you when
Your windows are down.)
I drove along thinking:
How long can we really be protected
From the dust of the world
This illusion of security will pop
With as much force
As the illusion of the state of Israel
Or us Americans

Running the world
So far my car is still driving
But will I reach a sign tomorrow
Which says: *Dead End*
Indicating
That we are reaching a path
On which we can walk no more??

Shame on Israel
Stings me like an insect bite
As I remember Ghada,
My Palestinian counterpart
After sitting in her home
And taking it as mine
And still, I don't use that word, shame.

Sham means there
Shamayim means sky
Over there in the sky
There is space
For all our ideas to roll and turn
And who knows,
Tomorrow
I may be walking
Rather than driving my car.

Edward Morin

FATHER HOLTSCHNEIDER CONSIDERS DR. NORMAN FINKELSTEIN'S TENURE

1. Furor Scholasticus

We hired him as a hot property.
His trailer, laden with publications,
radiated prestige which DePaul needed.
Recommendations and teaching record
shone like finest Tiffany jewelry.
Who cared if Gotham universities
denied him tenure? We missed that omen.
Six years with us, and his publications—
counting translations into foreign tongues—
outnumber those of my whole Arts faculty.
Lord save us, the mere mention of his name
makes plaster fall from my office ceiling.

He's a nice enough guy until he starts
talking about the Palestinians.
Then he becomes a bulldog who won't let go
of his bone. He told me he has been sharing
their miseries each summer in the West Bank.
I asked him why he sniffs out all that trouble.
He smiled and answered, "Because it's there."
Behind his growl I sensed compassion,
a strange hunger and thirst for justice.

Committees voted 9-3 and 6-0
to grant tenure; then an avalanche
of complaints accused administrators
and this son of holocaust survivors
of being anti-Semites. Embarrassment.
Norman's rival in Poli Sci asked

Harvard lawyer Alan Dershowitz
to find mistakes in Norman's publications.
He sent eighty pages called "faults and lies" —
none of it discredited Norman's work.
Alan's grudge was old news after Norman
exposed faked sources in Alan's book,
The Case for Israel, written by committee.
On Amy Goodman's radio program
Democracy Now, Norman told Alan:
"You don't even know what's in your own book."

2. Governance

Give me a break. My job as President
is to make DePaul the best Catholic
University in America.
We're already the largest. In my field,
Policy, good feelings and decorum
grease the chutes for donor contributions.
Samuel Johnson defined scholars as
"harmless drudges." They're the kind I like —
compulsives who just write history
and don't go rabble rousing on the road.

By speaking in high profile venues,
Norman gave us bad public relations.
I'm "Mr. Outside" at this institution
and can't stand to see our image tarnished.
Dr. Johnson said of free speech: "A man
may express any opinion, and any other man
may knock him down for it." Alan's crew tried.
I kept the decision out of their hands.

We Vincentians put great store in "personalism":
only persons have souls, every one matters
and needs respect (including all our donors
despite their intellectual limitations).

Vincentian Personalism would require
Norman to show respect even toward Alan.
He could have tried talking nicer to him
instead of launching his own Norman Conquest.

Why has controversy been the Catholic Church's
middle name? We need charity just to keep
from killing one another. Frankly,
our board, administrators, and core
faculty are corporate DePaul;
adjuncts, "tenure tracks," and grad assistants
just work here. I pray we all know our places.

3. Bon Voyage

Thank God we worked out a deal. For his office
and the year of classes to which he was entitled,
I gave what professionals expect:
praise and a long, paid leave—a bronze parachute.
He may do well on speaking tours, but complains
that our actions blackball him and he'll never
teach again on an American campus.
He loves to teach and students love him,
especially those who sat in at my office
and went on a ten-day fast for his sake.
Some wiseacres called me Pontius Pilate.

I wish Norman well. His case is not unique.
The 16th-century Augustinian scholar,
Fra Luis de Leon, ran afoul of the Inquisition
for saying the Latin Vulgate was
a poor translation of the Hebrew Bible.
The son of Jewish *conversos*, he turned
The Song of Songs into the vernacular.
It got an "R" rating, so he spent five
horrible years in the pen. Returning to

Salamanca, he began his first lecture
with the words "As we were saying yesterday . . ."

These days one doesn't find safe haven
such as Salamanca gave Fra Luis,
but Norman deserves a niche somewhere
in anyone's backyard except ours.

Samuel Hazo

SUFFER THE LITTLE CHILDREN

Just four months into history,
   Sarah speaks in key of squeaks
   while reaching for her rattle.
                        Nothing
   distracts her but a televised explosion,
   followed by screaming.
                        Her father
   mutes the screen.
                        The screams
   sound louder in silence.
                        Powdered
   by bomb dust, remnants
   of children litter a street
   in Qana.
         Rescuers bundle
   bodies and bits in oriental
   rugs for burial.
               I turn
   away to gaze at Sarah
   sucking on her rattle.
                     As image
   overlaps with image, bombdust
   seems to whiten her cheeks.
I make a face to see
   if she will laugh.
                  She waits
   until my face becomes my face
   again, then blooms into a grin.
The silence keeps on screaming.

Sharon Doubiago

PLAYING OSLO POOL
WITH MAHMOUD DARWISH

for Ryan, 1993
for Palestine

On our honeymoon we visited you in Paris, that picture
of my carrying you down the street in the Arab
     arrondissement. Your father
took Johnny down to the local bar to play pool
with Mahmoud Darwish. I was not invited.
Johnny didn't know who Mahmoud Darwish was
nor, really, the poet I am. But there over the pool table
the Voice of Palestine said to my men
"Yes, I know her work."

Sometime that week, your father came in from
     the Oslo Agreements
sat down at the little kitchen table and announced
"We just lost the war."

Still in diapers, you kept playing with your big red truck
     out on the balcony,
your nose running, mouth drooling, allergic to something
and that night had one of your infamous tantrums.
We were sleeping on the living room floor, twelve stories up,
     sniffling
and stuffed up too, that's how I knew the allergy
was from the toxic floor.

Your screaming goes on and on in the bedroom.
Your father has taken over from your mother, his voice rising
and rising. I'm afraid
he's going to snap (how can he not?) Backed-against-the-wall

he demands you *Stop it!* descending deeper
and deeper into his own hysteria. Into you
and all he's lost. Behind us lifetimes of mothers
letting Father take over. Behind me, behind you too,
the Cherokee forbade the father from ever disciplining the child
knowing too much father power
always turns toxic.

For a long time I lay there on that toxic floor
knowing the right thing
but unable to do it, imprisoned
in those lifetimes, wanting to honor his fatherhood, his home.
Finally, another unbearable scream of yours,
I barged through the door
to your beautiful mother prone on the bed, the Paris nightscape
in the big window silhouetting
your beautiful father on the end, beautiful you on his knees
in a confrontation only a crucifixion or nuclear meltdown
could resolve

I took you from your father, he
let me. Instantly, after hours of hysteria, you were
calm. Well, you seemed to sigh, it's about time.
What took you so long? Amazing
your sense of justice, your knowing
authority is not justice, not even your father. Amazing
you were still in complete faith
that right will come to your rescue, that right
will restore itself

The next morning, nauseated by what I had done to him
but elated and informed by what I had done for you
I apologized.
Your mother, almost always wise, diplomatically sighed,
    "You should have
knocked. Just asked 'Can I be of help?'"
Yes, of course, why didn't I think of that in my rush

to rescue you?
"But yes," she said, "I felt
just like Grandma lying there doing nothing
while her child is being abused."

Behind us lifetimes honoring old gods, allowing
their takeover, not knowing how
to honor and break simultaneously
the correct manners, our proper places, sacred rituals, the killers
in enforcement, the
Others. How to put it back together
righteously

I am saddened by the news of the great poet's death
the voice of your father's people, one half of you all
      the way back.
I've always expected that little mistake
—just one of the many we were and are bound to make—
would one day be corrected. Right
will restore itself, we will be introduced, I will say
I know your work Mahmoud Darwish. I will hear
him read

as I heard your cries that night
and though, insulting, incorrect, against the laws
finally acted

Maryna Ajaja

REPLY

> Write down that I am an Arab,
> that my grandfather's vineyards
> were stolen and all the Arab
> lands were stolen.
>
> And when I'm left to starve,
> I'll eat anything, even the flesh
> of those who stole our land.
>
> —Mahmoud Darwish, *Identity Card*

Write down that I am a Jew
from an oppressed people
now known as the oppressor.
Write down that I am a Jew
with brown hair and green eyes.
And for all the gold fillings
pulled and piled into mountains,
I am changing the landscape.
I offer irrigation and orange groves.
Write that I share the exile stance,
that refugee has always been my name.
That we share the same holy places
and the same word for peace.
Write down that I'm a Jew
living in Northwest America,
land of green and dampness,
and that I reject the desert,
the Promised Land.
I reject that law of both peoples —
An eye for an eye,
a tooth for a tooth.

I'd rather be mute and blind.
Write down that I'm a Jew
and reject the veil, the wig
and the male god who orders them.
I bet that bothers you.
I bet you don't like that!
And don't bother to write my name,
no mister, no missus.
I'm not interested in formalities,
your stalling tactics.

Write that this land
belongs to no one.
Only dust claims first ownership.
And over this dust
we erect a new landscape,
over the bones of Abraham,
over the bones of Mohammed's children.
Write down that I hate no one
and reject oppression.

I have walked through the orchards,
those lush landscapes,
and seen tractors roll down
aisles of gleaming fruit.
I've heard the prophets scream
from the roofs of Jerusalem.
I've heard all the dogmatic arguments
and prayers at the wall.
And for every passive Jew
who stood in the shower line—
I write this for you:
Hate begets hate
and religion is hypocritical,
pitting people against people.
And for every Arab
with a drawn knife,

with the same blood I have,
insist on justice
and be just yourself.

Yes, write at the top of the page
that I'm a Jew with
brown hair and green eyes.
Write that I'm a Jew
and that I don't hate anybody.
I have been hungry
but I would rather starve
than eat your flesh.

Naomi Shihab Nye

HELLO, PALESTINE

In the hours after you died,
all the pain went out of your face.
Whole governments relaxed
in your jaw line.
How long had you been away
from the place you loved best?
Every minute was too much.
Each year's bundle of horror stories:
more trees chopped,
homes demolished,
people gone crazy.
You'd turn your face
away from the screen.
At the end you spoke
to your own blood
filtering through a machine:
We'll get there again, friend.
When you died, your long frustration
zipped its case closed.
Everyone in a body is chosen
for trouble and bliss.
At least nothing got amputated, I said,
and the nurses looked quizzical.
Well, if only you had seen his country.

Carolyne Wright

ROUND: BEFORE THE START
OF THE LONG WAR

She knelt in the soil of Rafah, before
the armored bulldozer's advancing blade.
She wore fluorescent orange so even the gods
of the coming war could see her, young woman
holding a megaphone aloft in crossed sights
of the guard tank. The bulldozer driver
had orders — demolish the day's quota of homes
and thousand-year-old olive groves
that blocked the occupiers' rising wall.

She wore fluorescent orange, reflective stripes
brilliant as Joseph's coat as he knelt before
his brothers in a pit in the dirt of Dothan.
Raising the megaphone like a torch, she rose
with earth in the D9 bulldozer's advancing scoop
till she was eye-level with its cockpit.
There would be no accident in the guard tank's
gun sights, she was eye-to-eye with the D9 driver.

What did she say, lowering her megaphone
to him who had orders to knock down the village
doctor's home in the shadow of Gaza guard towers?
There would be no accident, but the driver
had his orders, dropped his eyes, dropped
the bulldozer's blade, her megaphone rolled away as
her foot caught in the toothed scoop, she slipped,
her shocked comrades in their own fluorescent vests
ran toward her screaming *No* as panic flashed

across her face, brilliant as tracer fire
bleeding each night in the Gaza sky.
Night in the D9 driver's eye, as thick
dirt pushed up by the advancing blade
poured over her, the 9-ton bulldozer rolled
over her. Stopped. Reversed. Rolled back.
Withdrew. Her comrades screaming threw themselves over
the broken form they dug from the packed earth's tracks.

Only darkness in her eyes rolled back, blood's
shocked petals spread over her face as if
to shield her from her own bloodsource as sobbing
praying friends cradled her body's ebb
and gods of the long war drew back on the village's
crumbling doorsteps. No light in the bulldozer
driver's eye, who'd witnessed everything from
his lofty cockpit: the orange-striped girl
tumbling from his sight-level like Joseph

into a pit in Gaza, her blood-brilliant
coat delivered unto her father, her mother
as the tank's and bulldozer's crushing treads
tracked back to the iron wall's perimeter
and drove off. No aid for the dying girl
as minutes before the ambulance arrived
grew to seem years across the iron wall where
she went on kneeling in the soil of Rafah.

Rachel Corrie
Rafah, Gaza Strip
16 March 2003

Rachel Corrie

E-MAIL TO HER MOTHER

February 27, 2003

Love you. Really miss you. I have bad nightmares about tanks and bulldozers outside our house and you and me inside. Sometimes the adrenaline acts as an anesthetic for weeks and then in the evening or at night it just hits me again—a little bit of the reality of the situation. I am really scared for the people here. Yesterday, I watched a father lead his two tiny children, holding his hands, out into the sight of tanks and a sniper tower and bulldozers and Jeeps because he thought his house was going to be exploded. Jenny and I stayed in the house with several women and two small babies. It was our mistake in translation that caused him to think it was his house that was being exploded. In fact, the Israeli army was in the process of detonating an explosive in the ground nearby—one that appears to have been planted by Palestinian resistance.

This is in the area where Sunday about 150 men were rounded up and contained outside the settlement with gunfire over their heads and around them, while tanks and bulldozers destroyed 25 greenhouses—the livelihoods for 300 people. The explosive was right in front of the greenhouses—right in the point of entry for tanks that might come back again. I was terrified to think that this man felt it was less of a risk to walk out in view of the tanks with his kids than to stay in his house. I was really scared that they were all going to be shot and I tried to stand between them and the tank. This happens every day, but just this father walking out with his two little kids just looking very sad, just happened to get my attention more at this particular moment, probably because I felt it was our translation problems that made him leave.

I thought a lot about what you said on the phone about Palestinian violence not helping the situation. Sixty thousand workers from Rafah worked in Israel two years ago. Now only six hundred can go to Israel for jobs. Of these six hundred, many have moved, because the three checkpoints between here and Ashkelon (the closest city in Israel) make what used to be a forty-minute drive, now a twelve-hour or impassible journey. In addition, what Rafah identified in 1999 as sources of economic growth are all completely destroyed—the Gaza international airport (runways demolished, totally closed); the border for trade with Egypt (now with a giant Israeli sniper tower in the middle of the crossing); access to the ocean (completely cut off in the last two years by a checkpoint and the Gush Katif settlement). The count of homes destroyed in Rafah since the beginning of this intifada is up around six hundred, by and large people with no connection to the resistance but who happen to live along the border. I think it is maybe official now that Rafah is the poorest place in the world. There used to be a middle class here—recently. We also get reports that in the past, Gazan flower shipments to Europe were delayed for two weeks at the Erez crossing for security inspections. You can imagine the value of two-week-old cut flowers in the European market, so that market dried up. And then the bulldozers come and take out people's vegetable farms and gardens. What is left for people? Tell me if you can think of anything. I can't.

If any of us had our lives and welfare completely strangled, lived with children in a shrinking place where we knew, because of previous experience, that soldiers and tanks and bulldozers could come for us at any moment and destroy all the greenhouses that we had been cultivating for however long, and did this while some of us were beaten and held captive with 149 other people for several hours—do you think we might try to use somewhat violent means to protect whatever fragments remained? I think about this especially when I see orchards and greenhouses and fruit trees destroyed—just

205

years of care and cultivation. I think about you and how long it takes to make things grow and what a labour of love it is. I really think, in a similar situation, most people would defend themselves as best they could. I think Uncle Craig would. I think probably Grandma would. I think I would.

You asked me about non-violent resistance.

When that explosive detonated yesterday it broke all the windows in the family's house. I was in the process of being served tea and playing with the two small babies. I'm having a hard time right now. Just feel sick to my stomach a lot from being doted on all the time, very sweetly, by people who are facing doom. I know that from the United States, it all sounds like hyperbole. Honestly, a lot of the time the sheer kindness of the people here, coupled with the overwhelming evidence of the willful destruction of their lives, makes it seem unreal to me. I really can't believe that something like this can happen in the world without a bigger outcry about it. It really hurts me, again, like it has hurt me in the past, to witness how awful we can allow the world to be. I felt after talking to you that maybe you didn't completely believe me. I think it's actually good if you don't, because I do believe pretty much above all else in the importance of independent critical thinking. And I also realize that with you I'm much less careful than usual about trying to source every assertion that I make. A lot of the reason for that is I know that you actually do go and do your own research. But it makes me worry about the job I'm doing. All of the situation that I tried to enumerate above—and a lot of other things—constitutes a somewhat gradual—often hidden, but nevertheless massive—removal and destruction of the ability of a particular group of people to survive. This is what I am seeing here. The assassinations, rocket attacks and shooting of children are atrocities—but in focusing on them I'm terrified of missing their context. The vast majority of people here—even if they had the economic means to escape, even if they actually wanted to give up resisting on their land and just leave (which appears to be maybe the less nefarious of Sharon's possible goals), can't leave. Because they can't even get into Israel to apply for visas, and because their destination countries won't let them in (both our country and Arab countries). So I think when all means of survival is cut off in a pen (Gaza) which people can't get out of, I think that qualifies as genocide. Even if they could get out, I think it would still qualify as genocide. Maybe you could look up the definition of genocide according to international law. I don't remember it right now. I'm going to get better at illustrating this, hopefully. I don't like to use those charged words. I think you know this about me. I really value words. I really try to illustrate and let people draw their own conclusions. I'm just thinking about that. If I'm really honest I won't talk about the power imbalance when people ask about Palestinian violence. I will talk about resisting genocide . . .

Rachel Corrie was a young activist from Olympia, Washington, U.S.A., who went to Palestine with a peaceful solidarity group. She was living with a Palestinian family, whose home was about to be demolished by the Israeli army, and died on March 16, 2003 under the treads of an Israeli bulldozer. We thank her parents, Craig and Cindy Corrie, for allowing us to print their daughter's writing.

Reja-e Busailah

IN MEMORY OF RACHEL CORRIE

He demolished Rachel's body
as you would demolish
a home with hearth and all;
like all children, when a child,
he may have had all the tenderness and charm

of a full grown butterfly.
He grew backward
he flattened her as he sang
along with the song of his towering engine,
crushed her effortlessly

as may a blind man
crush under his blind feet
the cricket singing his summer song
he crushed and sang confidently
emulating a predecessor of his

Singing *"Freude, Freude"*
as he shoved them into the oven,
both an element
alien to the primal law,
both the destructive element

which targets the bone marrow,
obstruction in the flow of the common stream,
both grew backward
back to the caterpillar phase.
He bulldozed her

as you would bulldoze
the wings of a honeysuckle

or laughter new-born
bathed in the fresh dew,
crushed her with a blind engine

of the sound ever so angry
of the looks ever so ugly
designed and built by Caterpillar.
Rachel's body is demolished,
her young bones crushed.

She came from far
seeking, unlike others,
no profit
no fame
no pleasure.

She came alone to shield from man's sorry touch
the pride of man's work through time,
the nest in which is born the will
to build another nest,
and another, and another down to times end

warmth of hearth and bed
bustle of child in laughter and in tears
labor within,
labor without
and sanctuary for ripe years;

And when he lunged with death at her
she looked him in the eye and stood her ground
she was not one of those who come
to fatten on a people's cream
only to abandon them at the hour of need—

Who will mourn Rachel Corrie
staring as much in death as in life?
the deathless fire that lights up the endless path,

the fragrance of the jasmine that knows all,
the blossom that carries the years to full term;

And as long as dreams are born
and the sun follows its westward course
and the shallow brook swells toward the sea,
as long as spring follows from winter
and man from awkward child

homes shall rise faster than they are razed
shall make life,
shall nurse and nourish life
and be the fast and sure bridge
for the procession of time.

Rachel's spirit shall not die
Rachel's spirit shall live
the patron saint of homes
as long as there are caterpillars
which give birth to butterflies.

At 23 years of age, Rachel Corrie was crushed to death by an Israeli-driven, American-built bulldozer as she was trying to stop the demolition of a Palestinian home on March 16, 2003.

VI

Judith A. Brice

QUESTIONS OF BETRAYAL

I

For a Jew there is a fundamental question:
"How can I believe in God?"
After Kristallnacht and Pogroms,
After the Boxcars,
After the six million slaughtered,
Snuffed out by tasteless gas,
Swallowed forever by fiery furnaces—
Furnaces belching Jew-dust over sparkling German towns:
(Towns at work to expunge each final smudge of Jew),
Jew-dust to breathe, to exhale, to dust off the mantle,
Jew-dust to contaminate the air.

Was it six million?

How to count each separate shtetl
Deleted from the map?
How to know each shivering woman
Forced naked to her grave?
How to count the Jew-dust flakes
Billowing brown into smoke?

Can we ever know
Each faceless soul,
Each desperate life,
Each girl sobbing in the rain?
How can we feel her, touch her?
How can we *make her* count?

For a Jew there is this essential question:
"Do I still believe in God"?

II

For a Jew there is yet another question:
"Can I believe in Love"?

Love for my neighbors,
Love for those I hate—
Members of Hesbollah or Hamas,
Now, during the bombings in Lebanon, Iraq,
And Afghanistan?
Can I feel the compassion and love I lost
After Kristallnacht
After the Boxcars
After my family was betrayed?

Will I listen now to cries of others?
Can I bear to hear *their* plight?

Dare I glance through rubble and see a mother in panicked fright?
Shall I bear witness to the nameless boy there crying?
Will I choose to make *him* count?

—For a Jew there is still this question:
Will I practice my belief in Love?

III

For a Jew there is yet the question:
"Can I believe in Light?"

A light for redemption, a light for forgiveness,
A light to shine on enemies and me alike,
To imbue each of us with hope?
For our sake, our world's sake,
Is there space enough for each
To have a home, a life, a love?

Or must we all continue to betray,
To kill, and *all* be killed, and *all* return to dust?

For a Jew there is but one last question:
"Is there a time for God, for Love, for Light?"

Kristallnacht—or the *Night of Broken Glass*, also known as
Reichskristallnacht, Pogromnacht, and *Novemberpogrome*—was
a pogrom or series of attacks against Jews throughout Nazi
Germany and parts of Austria on November 9 - 10, 1938

Willa Schneberg

AN ATTEMPT AT HASTENING
THE MESSIANIC AGE

*On August 21, 1969, Dennis Michael Rohan
committed arson at the al-Aqsa Mosque.*

I know every crevice of the al-Aqsa Mosque,
and the stone interior as intimately
as the skin of sheep I was paid to shear.

When God tells me what I must do
electric shocks explode through my body.

The pulpit inlaid with cedar
that the *imam* climbs every Friday
to indoctrinate the infidels
is hollow in the rear,
and perfect for my purpose.

Those venal fools who guard the mosques
do nothing except supply shawls
to bare shouldered girls.

They see another tourist
with a blonde crew cut
and let me snooze on their prayer rugs.

Soon the Temple will be rebuilt
to surpass its former glory.
I have all the necessary items.
In my stocking feet
I wrap my scarf saturated in benzene
around the kerosene container.
Just one match
will light His way.

Yasmin Snounu

PHOSPHOROUS HOLOCAUST

Tuesday, January 13, 2009

The Israeli escalation goes on;
no words adequately describe the holocaust
committed against Gaza's people by the so-called State
    of Israel.

In the seventeenth and eighteenth days of its war on Gaza,
the Israeli army continues bombing and shelling
areas that include homes with civilians in them.

Each day more children and women are killed.
Everyone is exposed to death here; nobody is safe.
You never know when your turn will come,
when death will knock out your life.

If you are lucky enough not to be hit by a heavy bomb,
then you will be trapped at home trying to calm and soothe
your hungry children who suffer from stomach pains
caused by lack of food, water, and sanitation.
Malnutrition and infectious diseases may carry them off.

The worst weapons Israel is using are phosphorous bombs,
which emit combustibles we cannot extinguish.
So most of the injured suffer from severe burns on face
    and body.
Phosphoric burns and emissions affect children horribly.

We have lost our habit of sleeping;
we've hardly slept since the beginning of the war.
If shells aren't targeting your house,

they're targeting your neighbors',
so you are threatened directly or indirectly.

These days, the only sound you can hear is
American-made F16s bombing and shelling;
at night tanks shoot and shell everything they pass;
devastation covers the Gaza Strip like never before.

A lot of people have left home to stay with relatives at their
    homes;
thinking they'd be safe, they later realize no place in Gaza
    is safe.
People are fleeing to nowhere; they are in a huge prison
controlled by the F16s, tanks, bulldozers and artillery.

To this moment, the number of martyrs numbers 980,
along with 4,418 wounded who wish they had died
rather than live with the afflictions they have received.

Gaza has been under fire for eighteen days,
no one is moving, the coming days are cloudy, uncertain,
and this holocaust will kill more people
unless the International Community takes real actions
to stop this brutal attack on Gaza.

Willa Schneberg

CONVERSATION IN CAESAREA

for Hannah Senesh

I

Hannah, perhaps we could've met
among the ruins
if the years weren't between us.
I would have listened
to you speak of the Land,
how the hammering, dredging,
sowing, fruit picking
plucks the strings of David's harp,
tears the yellow star
forever from our coats and
re-stitches it into the sky,
where above boulevards and dirt roads
full of Shabbat dinner *yehudim* stroll.
Even if we could have floated together
in your Mediterranean
before Caesarea became a tourist trap
and recognized that we both feel apart,
finding no one *to spread before him
the white cloth of heart and soul,*
we would not have been close,
because your poems are we and our,
mine, *I* and *their;*
you refused the Nazis' clemency,
wished to be shot without a blindfold,
while I want to die of old age.

II

In the *Jerusalem Post* is an article:
"A New Generation of Palestinian Martyrs,"
about children, young as nine,
in *Ketziot, Dahariya, Ansar 2,*
bound hand and foot, except
to eat or move their bowels —
no tent, no showers, no scribbled messages
allowed dispatch.

Hannah, sit across the table from me,
give me answers. If I were you,
I'd pull myself away from my desk. I know
the only poem not absurd is action.

In 1939, Hannah Senesh made aliyah to Palestine from Hungary. She was a poet and resistance fighter, who parachuted into Yugoslavia, and with the Partisans infiltrated her prior homeland. Her mission was to rescue Jews from Nazi-occupied Hungary. She was eventually captured by the Nazis, and shot to death. She was twenty-three.

Lahab Assef Al-Jundi

COLLATERAL SAVAGE

for Lebanon, 2006

Survivors of The Holocaust please
talk to me. Help me understand—
Do you sanction what's being done
in your names?

I thought your spirits
grew more gentle
having lived through the unspeakable.

Bombs are not less lethal or evil—
Stop being so deathly afraid
of *the other.*

A thousand eyes for an eye?
Children of The Holocaust
please do not lash out
as if you lost your sight.

Richard E. Sherwin

MY FRIENDS AND I

my friend can't sleep nights
dreams his family keeps calling him to save them
from the german furnaces
fertilizing europe with jewish ashes

he comes early sabbaths to synagogue
after me
saying i must be hoping to catch Gd
awake

me i'm trying to catch me awake
wake up says one lapel button
stop illusions says another
my hari krishna friend gives me

how can you live without illusions
asks my belgian diamond merchant friend

how do you wake up i ask
and why should i want to

he dreams reality
unable to sleep

the Lord's supposed not to slumber
and this is israel's redemption begun

who'd i be awoken
who'd we be
"one long war with breaks in between"
all our lives

jewhaters bombing our borders
Gdhaters stoking furnaces
i gave my soul to Gd
to wake and sleep at will
my first sergeant got my body
decades ago

no jonah no job no jesus

except on yom kippur

when all of us come for counting

Holocaust Day 2009

Scot Siegel

LUCKY STAR

Before the State of Israel
in the country of everlasting night
They became dust before they died
for a country of light, before it was . . .

They had no flag
        no song
        no homeland . . .

But an indigo shield arched over them
And now us, like a prayer

And a yellow star
emblazoned upon it

Gavriel Reisner (Ben-Ephraim)

TWO STORIES

My father no warning told a story I'd never heard

Our wedding spring of ___
Old Jaffa Hotel The Scotch House
"best restaurant in Israel"
Sixteen people on our honeymoon
A family affair
arriving in Bat Yam
a threadbare and emotional Tel Aviv town
Sephardi workers and Holocaust survivors.

My aunt Felah, with her enormous green eyes,
a natural blond
Marlene Dietrich reincarnated
as a coarse and great-breasted
Jewish waitress, running a worker's restaurant.

(She was angry at me once,
"no we're not professors," she said,
I forgot what I did,
But she held my mother during Nazi selections
Hiding a strong right arm).

On her balcony with no view at all
She made the heaviest of all cholents
Beans meat potatoes cooked for days
Served on a table laden with memory.

That's when it came like a wrecking ball
Not from the body of stories woven
The family mythology of Felix/Felek/Father
The small giant whose tales shadowed my schoolboy life
And distanced me from my slight existence.

Now came a completely new story,
How I resented the power of old friends
Hardly seen for 25 years
To call forth stories of endless consequence.

"When I came to Warsaw from the Russian army—it was
the end of '44—the Ghetto was a bombed-out shell, but I
found my old apartment building on Nalevska St. There
was a neighbor he recognized me, "Froyem, Froika" he
called—and he told me what happened to my family. The
Nazis came and took my not-so-old parents, my father who
loved *Shvitzbaths* and my mother who loved Chopin, and
my little brother Shmulik the tough blond lefty who'd
wear his worker's cap to the side, they took them up to the
roof and forced them at bayonet point to jump off. "That's
how they died, Froyem, that's how they died."

Just like that my father told a story he'd never told me
I blamed him for insensitivity, then,
but know now that such a story,
not contrived, pours forth when it will,
(the tale tells us when to tell it)
I couldn't get the images out of my mind,
People spilled like beasts on bloodstones
I walked around for days
in unknown modes without being.

Years later another haunting speech
Cast me once more from sight to thought.

In our new apartment overlooking the Valley of the Cross
We had an Arab-Christian contractor, Ilias Attiyeh, from
    Ramallah.
He had a large, slow earnest charm, a good man I thought.
When my wife miscarried, I told him. He cared—
    there was something about him,
I visited him once, met his wife, she had the same quality;

It was like that in Israel, during the charmed years
    between '67 and '73.
The Christian Arabs of Palestine,
There were many once in Ramallah, Bet-Jallah, Bet-Lehem.
They're mostly gone now.

He had some young painters working in our apartment,
Our aerie, above the beautiful valley where they cut
    the wood for Jesus' cross,
I enjoyed talking to them, talked to everyone then.

One sweet-tempered young man abruptly took a brush
    dripping with white paint
And said, "You wiped Palestine right off the map
    just like that," as he made a Stroke, a minor one, across
the side of the door frame.

I was speechless but now
In my muteness or dumbness his grief overtook me
He was a young man suspended in air
Just like my father identified
With his younger brother, independent Shmulik,
All of them falling, falling,
Falling with no comfort from the earth.

Hannah Stein

BODY PARTS

Outside a market, a foot
lies on the ground. An arm,
skin leathery and suntanned, or
slack, with blue cables of veins.
The freckled, the spotless,
the hairy, the smooth.

A rabbi in long coat and black hat
picks them up.
He will save them
for burial with the dead,
so that on the last day no one will arise
without feet, arms.

The rabbi puts them
in the plastic bag, mixes
defenders with attackers.
At the last day, all
will stand up together.

Samih al-Qasim

Excerpt: AFTER THE APOCALYPSE

I feel my limbs,
but cannot find them.
I implore my sense of sight,
but see nothing beyond a neutral grey.
Suddenly, warm radiates through the sand
crowding my spirit.
I discover my hands and legs,
there they are, familiar limbs,
assembling themselves into a heap of sand!
My body sees me.
Here I am, creating myself in my own image.
Here I am, the first human on another planet called:
Dayr Yasin,

One could say then that humanity
reconsiders itself,
reconsiders the laws, and the laws of the laws,
takes phenomena seriously,
in anticipation of what surprises the future holds
in the galaxy's enchanted whirl,
orbited by earthly satellites
gushing from wombs of volcanoes
to be grabbed immediately
by space scientists
who bless them with the loveliest names:
Lidice
Kufr Qasim
Sabra, Shatila,
My Lai.
One cannot help being astonished
at the breakdown of norms and mores,
at the simultaneous fall of all equations,

let alone fig trees, bonds, travel tickets, house arrests,
school and marriage certificates,
let alone global conventions: the Third World,
European Common Market, the Stock Market,
Alignment and Nonalignment, Nuclear Weapons, Disarmament,
and documents of death.

Come with me, bedouin girl,
you who have not yet spoken,
come, let's give names to new things,
they may give us back our own names in return.
In my name you rise from the dead.
In your name I make death acceptable,
a familiar morning greeting,
a bending over the neighbor's fence
to pluck a little rose for a tired lapel.
O virgin bedouin girl, with lips open,
but silent, you see everything
through the transparent wall of Apocalypse,
you bear on your shoulders the burden of everything:
storms, bloodstained hands, children's lips
still clutching their mother's severed breasts,
everything: trees twisted in the mud,
tall blackened buildings, broken windows,
charred skeletons sitting cross-legged
cigarette in hand, watching the TV set
continue its broadcast (live under the rubble)
of the emergency session
of the United Nations . . . etc. etc.

You see through the transparent wall
of Apocalypse sound mufflers on secret guns,
nickel handcuffs, police billy clubs, tanks,
tear gas bombs, demonstrations, burning car tires,
and bullets fired into the air,
apologizing to angels,
making their ways straight
to the school girls' breasts.

At this, international agencies would hurry
to quiet reactions and rumors
while the doleful, angry chorus
exercises its absolute freedom
in the biggest armed robbery
in history.

The present is an innocent lie.
To see the future we must consult the past—
a past ever-present before our eyes,
a mammoth octopus.

O virgin desert!
Here we are, sent by the heart and mind
on an official mission
to build the world anew.
To prepare it once again
for another Apocalypse!

Tree trunk against tree trunk,
stone next to stone,
thus the relationship takes form.
We begin from here
though doubts sometimes assail us.
Sometimes we'll miss one another,
but we won't be afraid to look behind.

Later,
new children will be born,
they'll ask their fathers sternly:
Why? For whom? When and how?
There won't be anyone to answer

except the ground waters singing:
I am grief! I announce my innocence!
I am desire! I enforce my authority!

I am love! I spread my sails on land
and scatter my seeds in the furrows of the sea.
I am hate! Your fire, your sacred fire!

Nothing remains the same.
In the long run, motion asserts itself,
erects new rules over the pure sands
now subject to factories' oil,
fires, the vomit of the sick,
and the wretched human din.

But after all this
there must be some recompense
for the children are about to go to school.
So let the storms subside a little
and the darkness lift itself off part of the road
for their sakes, for their sakes only,
for the sake of the children
going to school
after the Apocalypse!

Translated by Sharif Elmusa and Naomi Shihab Nye

VII

David Gershator

BAD WEATHER BLESSING

Thank god for bad weather
let it be a blizzard
let it freeze
let it thunder let it blow
they're predicting a storm
snow on the high points
from Galilee's hilltops
to the mountain peaks of Samaria
even the summits of Jerusalem

let children play with snow
keep people indoors
keep cars off the roads
keep people busy keeping warm
bad weather's a blessing
in the year of too many
stones bullets suicide bombers

let there be snow
on the mosques of rage
let weapons be frozen
let there be snow
on the synagogues of revenge
let everything remain
on icy hold
in nature's ceasefire

if bad weather could only last
for a year or two
it might cool things off
footprints in deep snow
might lead the way

let peace come from the North
with more bad weather
to cool things down
to give peace a chance
if there is half a chance
in any kind of weather

Atar Hadari

THEY ASKED US TO IMAGINE

They asked us to imagine for a moment
What peace would look like.
I closed my eyes and saw
The Allenby Bridge ablaze with business

At midnight or four am or just for breakfast
Women and children and motorbikes
Crossing from Israel to Jordan
Or the other way, just shopping—

It takes a long time, reverse
The natural motion is forward
Blowing up bridges is fast
The night of the bridges reversed takes decades

But I believe that light
One day will force my eyes open
And in the faltering night
I will see one or two, even three shoppers.

But the juggernaut takes time to stop
And meanwhile the cold cars roar past
The not yet abandoned checkpoint.
And no one carries bread across the Jordan.

But one crust of bread dropped
In that water would crumble
And make in its memory of bread
A new sea to wash every body clean of rubble.

And one little biscuit falls
Falls in the water of the Jordan
And who can forget what they so often held
A flower sweet as cinnamon but so hard to keep soft
    without opening your hand.

Miriam Stanley

WHAT A LAND TO SHARE

My nieces looked at the grottos in the steeps on limestone.
Touched the warm whirlpools off the Mediterranean.
Visited the bunkers empty in Golan Heights.
Flaked sunburn off peeling, teenage backs.
Got into the bus for the end of the tour.

After dinner, Katyushas hit Haifa.
My nieces heard bombs near their hotel.
They painted their toenails khaki green and emailed my sister.
Joked they were kidnapped to Lebanon.

I cook and watch the news.
Wolf Blitzer becomes wallpaper.
I read captions that Safad was hit.
Picture its artists and rabbis in basements.

My friend Farid emails that Gaza was engulfed.

Then sends a poem of his Jericho birth.
He asks if my nieces are still OK.
He has family in Lebanon.

His words are the murmur of the Kinneret.
Tonight, we will both cry over CNN,
our midsummer in a downpour.

Hadassah Haskale

GRAPES OF PEACE/INAAB SALAAM

There are grapes of wrath
Grapes of peace
I've tasted these
In Abu Dis.

Who casts a stone
Has lost his way
To the vineyard
Where peace clusters
Ripe for the picking

Through a window of faith
Of love that sees
Beyond the wall
Behind the bars
Prisoners waiting
To be born to light—
A man reaches:
'Taste this offering
from my vine.'

Who casts a stone
Has lost his way
To the vineyard
Where peace clusters
Ripe for the picking.

Say 'yes' to the hand
Extended in peace
And feast on grapes
Of Abu Dis,
INAAB SALAAM
INAAB ABU DIS
GRAPES OF PEACE.

Lahab Assef Al-Jundi

ANY REFUGEES IN THE WORLD

what is the first thing that comes to mind
when you hear of refugees?
what terror drove them out of their homes?
are they getting help?
what is being done for their safe return?

are Palestinians any different from any other refugees?
is it not their simple right
to return to the land they were driven from?

why are they being asked to settle
for money?
who designated the Palestinians as the chosen people
to carry the cross for a guilt-ridden West?
why do politicians tell them
too much time has passed
when their grievance
is with people who went back after 2000 years?

between continued warfare and annihilation
coexistence beckons
as the only
honorable
demographic.

time for peace
now.

Carol Alena Aronoff

THE OTHERS

He smiled as you passed him
on the street.

He soled your shoes,
sold you bread and rose petal jam.
His uncle was your father's friend.

His wife stood in line behind you,
head scarf clutched beneath her chin
like a crow
with tucked in wings uncertain
of her welcome or her place.

Her son looked up at you
and as you bent to meet his gaze,
solemn as black sapphire,
he touched the star of David
hanging from your neck.

You kissed his fingers.

Dana Negev

ALMOND BLOSSOMS

for M. Darwish

Dear Mr. Darwish
I too have sensed them
So light they
decorated my heart,
whispered secrets to me
As I played in the forest

Dear Mr. Darwish
I stumbled across a family
Who spoke not my language
when I was hiding amongst the trees,
they were having lunch
and I was running from
my own family who spoke only
of everyday things
and couldn't imagine
the secrets of the almond blossoms.

I stumbled across some
Of your people
And they were under the same
Almond grove
As I.

Dear Mr. Darwish
When I was older
I met my lover there
Under the almond grove
We came in spring
when the blossoms appeared

and covered my head and eyes
and white cotton dress
and bare feet.
My lover said I was like the blossoms
I gave him an orange. We danced
We heard the playing of a flute
And followed old paths
Where your people have walked too

Dear Mr. Darwish
The whiteness of these blossoms
Can blow all of us away
Look, they float so gently
In the spring breeze
They land on a sleeping farmer,
a woman hanging laundry on her porch,
a child strolling in the woods
and further,
They reach the sea,
the sleeping cities
and finally
They reach the moon.

I will be watching them
And I'll notice
That you or one of your people
are by my side
Together
We are watching the whiteness.

Ingrid Wendt

SURGEONFISH

What I don't tell Glen, when I respond to his prize-
    winning fourthgrade
novel about the Spined Avenger, could fill
another book

         and has done, and keeps on
      being rewritten, rewritten
               although it really can be

scary, I tell him, I know from experience, yes, that fish
really will attack, you've chosen your brave
protagonist well. But Ralph and I were swimming

too close, I tell him, to spawning grounds — eggs,
    or newly-hatched
young — or maybe that leveled-off part of the
reef was their own

         last night on TV, *the foreign*
      minister saying: For some, it's always been Land
      that must be defended; for others, it's Life;

           and the surgeonfish,

two of them, named for the bright orange, scalpel-sharp
fin at the base of the tail, striking
from out of the blue, head on, then swerving:

          flak glancing the whole

length of our bodies, again and again. We must have looked
    funny,

flailing, thrashing the surface, like runners dodging a sniper,
like puppets unstrung.

But they were beautiful. That's
what we'd come for (such color!) the neon

indigo stripes of the black-scaled surgeonfish, neon
indigo edging the top and bottom black fins, edging the tail;
that pectoral fin, close to the gills: such a bright daffodil
sun! And this just one of so many others named in my book
and on Glen's video game. (They're real!) And here we swam
(I draw for him, his carpet our sand): the Gulf of Aqaba,
Gulf of Suez, around the tip of the Sinai

>   *behind us, that manystoried*
>   *mountain, the sacred remains of Saint Catherine,*
>   *somewhere the spot where Moses received God's Law*

we swam,

>   *behind us, Magic Lake, not far inland: the whitest sand,*
>   *the water a turquoise like nothing we'd ever seen, we posed*
>   *for photos*

Glen, your resolution, I tell him, is wonderfully
balanced. Mature: the way the Spined Avenger saves
the reef from Scarface, the shark: without

fighting. They sign an agreement.

>   *What is the whole, or even half of the story?*
>   *Our guide, Mr. Jamal, in the last, the Six-Day War,*
>   *fought at Magic Lake; where we posed, he saw men fall.*

I don't say Israel. Egypt. Anwar Sadat. Rabin.
Mr. Jamal, our guide, didn't use wet suit or fins.
The currents were strong. Only an arm away

to our right, the reef dropped off into darkness.
Down, down, two thousand feet down.
And all we could see was beauty.

Miriam Stanley

MAKING LOVE IN METULA

Making love in a village, a clump of houses, a compound
   on a border town,
minutes from Lebanon, meters from war. So close, *katyushas*
   flew over and hit Kiryut Shmona, instead.

Embracing on the edge of pear trees and craters,
with plastic slides for children and soldiers driving south.

kissing while
men pick apples,
teachers recite,
a sergeant learns a poem,
uzis sag shoulders in buses,
I talk to elders about kibbutzim, they regret
that the children lived apart.

Cuddling near a tank painted day glow,
with a teal stencil of a peace sign on its armor

holding hands, joining shadows, inside
the basement with reinforced walls.

Violence just for greed, just for lust,
not to save one's own life, not to save one's baby,
is *osur*

The aloe in springtime blooms,
hyacinth flowers skirt the yard.
war is a subject that Metula hates

osur: Hebrew meaning *forbidden*

248

Monica Raymond

IN CANA

The Lebanese spelled it with a q, without the u.
Qana. That town where John said Jesus at a wedding
turned water into wine. The other gospels missed it.
They caught other miracles, but they missed that first miracle.
The guest said "You're not like the others, who just serve good
wine till we're drunk." Later Jesus said "I bring not peace
    but the sword."

But in that first miracle, there was nothing of sword.
It's important you understand this, you
apocalyptic idiots, Muslim, Christian, and Jew. A good
party, that was all—people dancing those wedding
dances, lifting a chair, like they still do, a miracle
they can get it up there without dropping it,

or, if they do drop it, without killing whoever's in it.
But it's family they love there, so if they do a sword
dance, it's just clacking them together like the Morris men,
    minor miracle
of coordination. At the Revels, they clacked so hard—you
should have seen!—they broke the blade. At a wedding,
that would probably be bad luck. It might be good

to leave the swords out of it for good.
That's a disarmament proposal, what do you think of it?
What if we acted as if the whole world were a wedding
with good wine till the end? What if you left your sword
at the door and never retrieved it? And you
just kept dancing and drinking all night, like that first miracle

and the wine never got less good—that would be a miracle.
You know I'm not just talking about the wine being good.

I'm writing a little parable or a sermon for you.
Yes, a dead prophet is not the only one who can do it.
I'm saying we've seen what comes of bringing the sword.
Now let's bring a covered dish, and get back to the wedding.

I like to think that maybe it's a wedding
of people from different sides, ordinary miracle—
two black-browed lovers, aflame like flowering swords.
Gladiola. Bird of paradise. What looks like a knife-edge
   sheathe till it
        unfurls in good
blossom. The angels each holding a stem of it
at the door of the fiery world, and they beckon to you.

They hold the flaming sword to protect the wedding,
and they want to include you in this miracle.
Not blood, but good wine that pours. Let us dream of it.

Mike Maggio

SUNDAY MORNING—AMMAN

Here in Amman
the church bells ring
there are Christian people here
they are our brothers
they are *ibn-khal*
Here in Amman
on al-Farabi Street
amid umbrellas and tea boys
and photocopy machines
there are Palestinian people here
they have come to renew their lives
with passport, ID and staff in hand
and amber garments the color of time
they are autumn leaves
thrown on the wind
they are our brothers
they are *ibn-ard*

Here in Amman
the muezzin calls
there are Muslim people here
from minaret to minaret
a chorus of voices
touches the soul
from steeple to steeple
a chorus of bells
gathers the souls
bells and voices
mingling
rising over the city
crying out to God
and the occupied land

and holy Jerusalem
where Christians and Muslims
Palestinians alike
and Jews on the West Bank
they are all *ahl-kitab*
Jews on the occupied West Bank
they are our brothers
they are *ibn-'am*

ibn-khal: maternal cousin; Muslims refer to Christians in this manner

ibn-ard: wanderers; literally, sons of the earth

ahl-kitab: People of the Book

ibn-'am: paternal cousin; Muslims refer to Jews in this manner

Naomi Shihab Nye

SHOULDERS

A man crosses the street in rain,
stepping gently, looking two times north and south,
because his son is asleep on his shoulder.

No car must splash him.
No car drive too near to his shadow.

This man carries the world's most sensitive cargo
but he's not marked.
Nowhere does his jacket say FRAGILE,
HANDLE WITH CARE.

His ear fills up with breathing.
He hears the hum of a boy's dream
deep inside him.

We're not going to be able
to live in this world
if we're not willing to do what he's doing
with one another.

The road will only be wide.
The rain will never stop falling.

BIOGRAPHICAL NOTES

Khaled Abdallah, born in Deir el Balh in Gaza in 1970, has published two collections of poems, *FM*, which won the 2001 AM Qattan Foundation poetry prize, and *Dar Al-Adaab* (Beirut, 2002). He lives in Paris.

Adonis (Ali Ahmad Said Esber) is a Syrian poet and essayist who led the modernist movement in Arabic poetry during the second half of the 20th century. He has written more than fifty books of poetry, criticism and translation in Arabic, including the pioneering work *An Introduction to Arabic Poetics*. In 2010, *Adonis: Selected Poems,* translated by Khaled Mattawa, was published by Yale University Press. He moved to Lebanon in the 1960s, to Syria in the 80s, finally to Paris, where he now lives.

Nitza Agam has a BA from Hebrew University in Jerusalem and Masters degrees in English and Comparative Literature from San Francisco State University. Her essay, "I Remember the Ocean," was published in *Bridges: A Jewish Feminist Journal* (Volume 14, Number 1, Spring 2009), and the poems "On a Tour-bus in Jerusalem" and "A Black and White Photo." in *Poetica: Reflections of Jewish Thought* (July and March 2007).

Dr. Ada Aharoni, founding president of International Forum for the Literature and Culture of Peace (IFLAC), writes in English, French and Hebrew. She has published twenty-six books, which have been translated into seventeen languages. She received a M.Phil in English Literature from London University and a PhD from Hebrew University, Jerusalem. Ada has received international poetry and literature prizes and was elected one of the best "Hundred Global Writer Heroines." Her work has been set to music and performed live in concert and recorded, most recently in 2011 with the CNY Jazz Orchestra.

Maryna Ajaja, born in Los Angeles, for the last twelve years she has made her home in Seattle and worked as a film programmer for the Seattle International Film Festival specializing in Eastern/Central European, Russian and Middle Eastern film. She has a BA in Literature from Evergreen State College, Olympia, Washington.

Carol Alena Aronoff, PhD is a psychologist, teacher and writer. Her poetry has appeared in numerous literary journals. She received a prize in the Common Ground poetry contest judged by Jane

Hirshfield and is a Pushcart Prize nominee. Her book, *The Nature of Music*, was published in 2005, *Cornsilk* in 2006, and *Her Soup Made the Moon Weep* in 2007. *Blessings From an Unseen World* is forthcoming.

Seema V. Atalla currently writes, translates and teaches in southern California. Her poetry and translations have appeared in several journals and anthologies, including *A Crack in the Wall: New Arab Poetry* (2001); *The Poetry of Arab Women: A Contemporary Anthology* (2001); and *We Begin Here: Poems for Palestine and Lebanon* (2007). Her article "Texts of Exile: Palestinians and the Promised Land" appeared in the *UCLA Journal of Middle Eastern Studies.*

Helen Bar-Lev, New York born, has lived in Israel for over forty years. She won the Amy Kitchener International Senior Poet Laureate award in 2009. She is senior editor of Cyclamens and Swords Publishing, and a well known Israeli artist who has held over eighty exhibitions around the globe. She is poetry editor for *Presence: An International Journal of Spiritual Direction* and contributing editor for *SKETCHBOOK, A Journal for Eastern and Western Short Forms.*

Rachel Barenblat was ordained a rabbi in January 2011 through ALEPH: the Alliance for Jewish Renewal. She holds an MFA from the Bennington Writing Seminars and is author of 4 chapbooks of poetry. Her first book-length collection, *70 Faces: Torah poems*, was published by Phoenicia in 2011. Her poems have appeared in a variety of journals, among them *The Jewish Women's Literary Annual* and *The Texas Observer*. Since 2003 she has blogged as *The Velveteen Rabbi;* she lives with her husband and son in western Massachusetts.

Ellen Bass's poetry books include *The Human Line* (Copper Canyon Press) and *Mules of Love* (BOA Editions). Her poems have been published in *The Atlantic Monthly, The Kenyon Review, American Poetry Review, The Sun, The New Republic*, and many other journals. Her nonfiction books include *The Courage to Heal and Free Your Mind.* She teaches in the MFA poetry program at Pacific University.

Grace Beeler is the granddaughter of Holocaust survivors from Vienna, Austria. She is the author of the chapbook, *A Lineage of Light.* Her work has appeared in *Mothering Magazine, Poetica Magazine, New Verse News*, and the anthology, *A Chaos of Angels*, among others.

Elana Bell has received grants and fellowships from the Jerome Foundation, the Edward Albee Foundation and the Drisha Institute. Her work has appeared in *CALYX, the Bellevue Literary Review,*

Storyscape and *Clamor,* among others. Elana has led creative writing workshops for women in prison, for educators, and for under served high school students in Israel, Palestine and throughout New York City. She is writer-in-residence for the Bronx Academy of Letters. Her manuscript *Eyes, Stones* won the 2011 Walt Whitman Award from the Academy of American Poets, to appear in 2012 from LSU Press.

Yael Ben-Israel was born in Jerusalem in 1982, and has lived there since. She has studied Arabic and literature and is currently working towards a PhD in literature at Hebrew University, Jerusalem. Previously published poems include "Doorways" in *Wazee,* "Foreign Languages" and "Pasha's" in *The Texas Observer,* and "Good Genes" in *Open Windows III,* an anthology of poetry, fiction and essays.

Tom Berman, a member of Kibbutz Amiad in the Upper Galilee, Israel, for over fifty years, is a scientist. Most of his research has been focused on the Sea of Galilee. He grew up in Glasgow, Scotland, having arrived there at age five from Czechoslovakia with the Kindertransport in 1939. He was Editor-in-Chief of the annual *Voices Israel* poetry anthology from 2003 to 2006.

Rick Black, book artist and poet, is the owner and founding editor of Turtle Light Press, a small press dedicated to books, fine art cards and photography. For six years, he lived in Israel, first studying Hebrew literature at Hebrew University and subsequently working as a journalist in the Jerusalem bureau of *The New York Times.* An international prize-winning haiku poet, he has written and handcrafted a chapbook, *Peace and War: A Collection of Haiku from Israel.*

Gloria Bletter is a retired lawyer concerned about human rights abuses. She visited the West Bank in 2002; her article, "Israel's Impunity under International Law," was published in *Peace Review* (March 2003). She obtained an MA in Creative Writing after retiring from her law practice and has taught poetry to adults learning English.

Judith Brice, a former psychiatrist, credits much of her inspiration to her past work with patients, to her own experiences with illness, to her love of nature, and to her strong feelings about politics. Her work has been published in several newspapers, reviews and anthologies including the *Pittsburgh Post-Gazette,* the *City Paper* (of Pittsburgh), the *Paterson Literary Review, Poesia* and *The Lyric.* Her poem "Questions of Betrayal" is part of the permanent archives of the Holocaust Memorial Center in Farmington Hills, Michigan.

Reja-e Busailah has been blind since infancy. At age seven he and his family were force marched by Zionist forces from Lydda, Palestine into exile. He was educated in Cairo and earned a PhD in English from New York University. He is the author of a collection of poems, *We Are Human* (1985). His poetry has appeared in *The Ordeal* and in *Arab Studies Quarterly*. He taught for thirty years at Indiana University, Kokomo, and is now a retired professor working on his childhood memoir.

Rachel Corrie (1979 - March 16, 2003) was an American member of the International Solidarity Movement (ISM) killed in the Gaza Strip by an Israel Defense Forces (IDF) bulldozer while in front of a Palestinian's home as a human shield attempting to prevent the IDF from demolishing the home. The IDF stated that the death was due to the restricted view from the IDF Caterpillar D9 bulldozer driver, while members of the ISM said "there was nothing to obscure the driver's view." A student at Evergreen State College in Olympia, Washington, she had traveled to Gaza during the Second Intifada.

Mahmoud Darwish (1942-2008) was born in Berweh near Acre, Palestine, which Israelis razed after the 1948 war. He lived as a refugee, joined the Communist Party, and experienced constant harassment, repression and imprisonment. He edited the Galilee newspaper *Al-Ittibad (Unity)*. In 1971 he moved to Beirut, where his reputation as the foremost poet of the resistance continued. He produced thirty volumes of poems, some of which are set to music as emblems of Palestinian struggle. He moved to Paris where he edited the literary review, *Al-Karmel*. His poems have been translated into English, most recently by Fady Joudah.

Joan Thaler Dobbie's parents were Viennese Jewish holocaust survivors. She was born in Switzerland, raised in Upstate New York, lives in Eugene, Oregon. Joan teaches Hatha yoga, has an MFA in Creative Writing from the University of Oregon, and has published several chapbooks and prize-winning poems. She co-wrote and edited *Before Us, Studies of Early Jewish Families in St. Lawrence County* and *Life Stories of the Old and Young*. Her work appears in many poetry magazines and anthologies, including the award winning, *Looking For Home, Women Writing about Exile* (Milkweed Editions, 1990).

Charles Doria is an American poet and translator who studied comparative literature at Harvard and SUNY Buffalo. He is publisher/editor of Assembling Press, and has himself published three books of poetry, *The Game of Europe*, *Short*, and *Shorter*. His books of translations include *Origins: Creation Texts from the Ancient Mediterranean* and *The Tenth Muse: Classical Drama in Translation* (Ohio University Press, 1980).

Sharon Doubiago's *Love on the Streets, Selected and New Poems, 2008,* received the Glenna Luschei Distinguished Poet Award and was a finalist for the Paterson Poetry Prize. She has published three memoirs, two dozen poetry books, and over a hundred essays. Her story collection, *The Book of Seeing With One's Own Eyes,* is on the Oregon Culture Heritage list. She holds 3 Pushcart Prizes, the Oregon Book Award for Poetry (for *Psyche Drives the Coast*) and a California Arts Council Award. Her book-length poem, "Mi Nazarene," was written for her Palestinian grandson, born the night the Gulf War started.

Sharif Elmusa was born in Palestine and came to the US in 1971. He obtained a PhD in urban studies and planning from M.I.T. in 1986. His poems have been published in several periodicals and in the *Anthology of Arab-American Poetry*. He participated in initial selections for the *Anthology of the Literature of the Arabian Peninsula* He lives in Washington, DC.

Amal Eqeiq is a native Palestinian born in the city of Al-Taybeh. She is a PhD. candidate in Comparative Literature at University of Washington, where she is also a teaching assistant in English and Comparative Literature. Amal's latest publication "Louder than the Blue I.D.: Palestinian Hip Hop in Israel" came out in *Displaced at Home: Palestinians in Israel: Gender and Ethnicity,* edited by Rhoda Kanaaneh and Isis Nusair (SUNY, 2010).

Merle Feld has written a memoir, *A Spiritual Life: Exploring the Heart and Jewish Tradition*, and a poetry collection, *Finding Words*. Her plays include *Across the Jordan* and *The Gates are Closing.* Merle organized and facilitated Israeli-Palestinian dialogue during the first Intifada, served at Seeds of Peace, helped staff a Rabbis for Human Rights mission to Israel, traveled to the former Soviet Union through Project Kesher, and is Founding Director of the Albin Rabbinic Writing Institute. She lives and works with husband Rabbi Edward Feld in Western Massachusetts.

Ruth Fogelman, a long-time resident of Jerusalem's Old City, won the Reuben Rose Poetry Competition, 2006 and was commended winner of the John Reid Traditional Poetry Competition in 2007. Her full poetry collection, *Cradled in God's Arms*, was released in 2009. She is author of *Within the Walls of Jerusalem—A Personal Perspective.*

Her writing and photography appear in anthologies and journals in Israel, the US and India. Ruth leads the Pri Hadash Women's Writing Workshop in Jerusalem and holds a Masters Degree from the Creative Writing Program of Bar Ilan University. A new chapbook of her Jerusalem poetry is forthcoming.

C.B. Follett won the 2001 National Poetry Book Award for *At the Turning of the Light* (Salmon Run Press). She has three other published poetry collections, the latest being *And Freddie Was My Darling*, (Many Voices Press, 2009). She has been widely published nationally and internationally, is included in many anthologies, and has received many contest honors. Five poems have been nominated for a Pushcart Poetry Prize and she has had three nominations as an individual poet.

David Gershator, born on Mount Carmel in British Mandated Palestine, taught Humanities at Rutgers, Brooklyn College, CUNY, and the University of the Virgin Islands, St. Thomas. He edited the Downtown Poets Co-op in the '70s and '80s, and is currently Associate Editor of *Home Planet News*. He received a National Endowment for the Humanities fellowship and a NY State Creative Artists' grant. He translated and edited *Federico García Lorca: Selected Letters* (New Directions) and co-authored 6 picture books for children. His poetry books include *Play Mas* and *Elijah's Child*.

Reuven Goldfarb co-founded and edited *AGADA*, the illustrated Jewish literary magazine, taught English at Oakland's Merritt College. His poems, stories and essays have appeared in many periodicals and anthologies, and have won various awards. Goldfarb moved to Israel in 1999, to Tzfat, a mountain village in Upper Galilee.

Atar Hadari was born in Israel, raised in England, and studied poetry and playwriting with Derek Walcott at Boston University. His *Songs from Bialik: Selected Poems of Hayim Nahman Bialik* (Syracuse University Press, 2000) was short-listed for the 2001 American Literary Translator's Association Award, and *Poetry Magazine* devoted nineteen pages to his translation of the Hebrew epic, "Lives of the Dead." His poems have recently won the New England Poetry Club's Daniel Varoujan Award and Grolier poetry prize.

Marian Haddad is a poet, writer, manuscript and publishing consultant, private writing mentor, visiting writer, lecturer and creative workshop instructor. Her poetry collections include *Wildflower. Stone.* (Pecan Grove Press, 2011), *Somewhere between Mexico and a*

River Called Home (Pecan Grove Press, 2004), and a chapbook, *Saturn Falling Down* (2003). She has taught creative writing at Our Lady of the Lake and Northwest Vista College, and International and American Literature at St. Mary's University. She is writing a collection of essays about growing up Arab-American in a Mexican-American border town.

Sam Hamod has published poetry about Palestine and the Middle East since the 1960s. The author of *Dying with the Wrong Name* (1980), he was nominated for a Pulitzer Prize in Poetry and has published ten collections, most recently *Just Love Poems for You* (2006). His work appeared in over two hundred anthologies worldwide, including *We Begin Here: Poems on Palestine and Lebanon* and *Not Surrender: Poems on Palestine*. He has taught at Writers' Workshops of the University of Iowa and at Princeton, as well as at University of Michigan and Howard University.

Hadassah Haskale's writing has appeared in journals and anthologies in the US, Israel, Britain, and Sweden. Hats she has worn include poet, psychologist, teacher, editor, writer and translator. In Israel, her primary home since 1973, she is currently concerned with grass roots promotion of peace, interfaith dialogue and the protection of a local natural open space. Her most recent book is *Wayfaring* (2007).

Mahmoud Abu Hashhash was born in the al-Fawar refugee camp, Hebron, in 1971. He has a degree in English language and literature from Birzeit University. Published in many magazines and journals including *Banipal*, he is the author of a poetry collection entitled, *Waja'a al-Zujaj [The Pain of the Glass]* (2001) and an article "On the Visual Representation of Martyrdom in Palestine," *Third Text* (2006). He is an editor at the Palestinian House of Poetry, and director of the Program of Culture and Arts at the Qattan Foundation in Ramallah.

Samuel Hazo, founding director of the International Poetry Forum in Pittsburgh and Professor at Duquesne University, earned his BA from the University of Notre Dame, an MA from Duquesne University, and a PhD. from the University of Pittsburgh. Once a Marine Corps captain, he is a prolific producer of poetry, fiction, essays, translations and plays. His book *Just Once* received the 2003 Maurice English Poetry Award. His most recent book is *Like a Man Gone Mad: Poems for a New Century* (2010). A National Book Award Finalist, he has eleven honorary doctorates and was Pennsylvania's first State Poet between 1993 and 2003.

Dafna Hornike was born and raised in Beer-Sheva in the Negev Valley. She currently lives in Ithaca, New York, where she dedicates her time to studying for a PhD in Spanish at Cornell University, focused on borders and connections between subjectivity and space as seen in Latin American literature. She has an MA from Calgary University and a BA from the Hebrew University, Jerusalem, which makes her research interest not merely theoretical.

Salma Khadra Jayyusi was born in Palestine of a Palestinian father and Lebanese mother. She grew up in Acre and Jerusalem, graduated from the American University of Beirut and the University of London. She has lived in nine countries including the US, becoming one of the Arab world's most distinguished literary personalities widely known for her poetry, literary criticism, scholarship and publishing programs. She has published two collections of poetry, *Trends* and *Movements in Modern Arabic Poetry*, as well as numerous articles and studies. She founded and directed the Project of Translation from Arabic (PROTA) for the translation of Arabic literature into English.

Lahab Assef Al-Jundi was born and raised in Damascus, Syria, attended The University of Texas, Austin, graduating as an electrical engineer. His poetry has appeared in numerous magazines, journals and anthologies. His first collection, *A Long Way*, was published in 1985. His new book, *No Faith At All,* is forthcoming from *Pecan Grove Press*.

Sami Al Jundi, a Palestinian living in Jerusalem, spent ten years in jail after the bomb he and his school friends were making went off in his bedroom, killing one friend, injuring himself and another. In prison, he met other activists, studied the classics, and even befriended a few Jewish Israeli political prisoners. Upon his release he established an organization aimed at bringing Palestinian and Israeli teens together with respect, tolerance and dialogue. His memoir, *The Hour of Sunlight* (Nation Books, 2011), co-authored with film maker and human rights advocate, Jen Marlowe, describes his journey from militant to advocate of nonviolence.

Christi Kramer, born in northern Idaho, holds an MFA from George Mason University and is currently a doctoral candidate at the University of British Columbia. Her poetry can be found in *The Enpipe Line; Foreign Policy in Focus; Sojourner's Magazine; Beltway Quarterly; Best New Poets 2007; Practice New Writing + Art;* and Lost Horse Press's anthology *I Go to the Ruined Place: Contemporary Poems in Defense of Global Human Rights.*

Judy Kronenfeld is the author of two books and two chapbooks of poetry, the most recent being *Light Lowering in Diminished Sevenths*, winner of the 2007 *Litchfield Review* Poetry Book Prize. Her poems, short stories and personal essays have appeared in numerous journals and anthologies. She is author of a critical study, *King Lear and the Naked Truth* (Duke University Press, 1998), and Lecturer Emerita in the Department of Creative Writing at the University of California, Riverside, where she taught for twenty-five years.

George Khoury, a Nakba survivor from Birzeit, Palestine, attended schools in Jordan and Egypt before emigrating to the U.S., where he received an engineering degree from the University of Detroit and an MBA from Central Michigan University. He translated many technical manuals for heavy machinery and autos from English into classical Arabic. He edits *The Birzeit Newsletter*, journal of the Birzeit Society, dedicated to preserving Palestinian culture. He edited the collected poems in Arabic of Diaspora poet Diab Rabie, entitled *Shetharat El-Rabie* (The Birzeit Society, 2010).

Joy Ladin holds the David and Ruth Gottesman Chair in English at Stern College of Yeshiva University. Early books include *The Book of Anna, Transmigration, Psalms, Wipf & Stock*. Her writing has been widely published in *Parnassus: Poetry in Review, Prairie Schooner, North American Review* and *Southwest Review.* She was a Fulbright Scholar at Tel Aviv University in spring 2002 at the height of a cycle of suicide bombings and Israeli army reprisals.

Mike Maggio has published fiction, poetry, travel and reviews in *Potomac Review, Pleiades, Apalachee Quarterly, The L.A. Weekly, The Washington City Paper, Gypsy, Pig Iron,* and *DC Poets Against the War.* His books include the audio collection, *Your Secret is Safe With Me* (Black Bear Publications, 1988); *Oranges From Palestine* (Mardi Gras Press, 1996); a book of short fiction entitled, *Sifting Through the Madness* (Xlibris, 2001); and a poetic critique of the Bush Administration entitled, *deMOCKcracy* (Plain View Press, 2007). He lives in Herndon, Virginia.

Peter Marcus has poems published in *The Southern Review, Antioch Review, Southwest Review, Crab Orchard Review, Poetry, Ploughshares, AGNI, Boulevard, Iowa Review, Shenandoah, Willow Springs, Prairie Schooner, Notre Dame Review, Quarterly West, Witness*; in the anthology *I Go to the Ruined Place: Contemporary Poems in Defense of Global Human Rights* (Lost Horse Press, 2009), and others. *Dark Square* was published by Pleasure Boat Studio in fall 2011. His upcoming work will appear in *Gargoyle, The Cafe Review* and *Alimentum.*

Susan Martin is a retired English and creative writing teacher. She has published short fiction and poetry in several anthologies, literary magazines and online sites. She was recently awarded third prize for her poem "First Lady" in the *Women in 2009* poetry contest. One of her poems appears in the Spring 2012 issue of *Poetica Magazine*.

Rochelle Mass, Canadian born translator and editor, emigrated with her family to Israel in 1973. After living in a Kibbutz in the Jezre'el Valley for twenty-five years, she now lives on the western flank of the Gilboa Mountains in the same valley. Her work has been widely published in journals and anthologies. She has published three poetry collections, her latest is *The Startled Land* (Wind River Press). Twice a Pushcart nominee, twice short-listed by the BBC, she took first and second prize in the Reuben Rose Poetry Competition in past years and, most recently, first prize and two honorable mentions.

Khaled Mattawa was born in Benghazi, Libya in 1964, and immigrated to the US in his teens. He is the author of four books of poetry: *Ismailia Eclipse* (Sheep Meadow Press, 1995), *Zodiac of Echoes* (Ausable Press, 2003), *Amorisco* (Ausable Press, 2008), and *Tocqueville* (New Issues Poetry & Prose, 2010). He has translated books by Arab poets into English, and co-edited *Post Gibran: New Arab American Writing*. Mattawa was recipient of the 2010 Academy Fellowship from the Academy of American Poets. He is Associate Professor of English at the University of Michigan, Ann Arbor.

Philip Metres has written a number of books, most recently the chapbook, *abu ghraib arias* (Flying Guillotine, 2011), *To See the Earth* (Cleveland State University Poetry Center, 2008), and *Behind the Lines: War Resistance Poetry on the American Homefront since 1941* (University of Iowa Press, 2007). His work has appeared in *Best American Poetry* and *Inclined to Speak: Contemporary Arab American Poetry* and has garnered an NEA, four Ohio Arts Council Grants, and the Cleveland Arts Prize in 2010. He teaches at John Carroll University in Cleveland, Ohio.

David Miller is an American writer working in various forms from poetry to travel writing. He is the founding editor of *The Traveler's Notebook* and senior editor of *Matador*. He lives with his wife and daughter in El Bolsón, a small town in Patagonian Argentina.

Edward Morin has had poetry in *Hudson Review, Ploughshares, Prairie Schooner*, and in his collections *Labor Day at Walden Pond* (1997) and *The Dust of Our City* (1978). He edited and co-translated *The Red*

Azalea: Chinese Poetry since the Cultural Revolution (University of Hawaii Press, 1990) and a book-length poetry manuscript by Cai Qijiao. His co-translations of Arabic poetry have appeared in *Connotations Press* and *The Dirty Goat.*

Bonnie J. Morris is a women's studies professor at George Washington and Georgetown Universities, the author of nine books, two on Jewish women's history in America. For almost twenty years she facilitated Jewish women's gatherings at the Michigan Women's Music Festival; leading for ten, the lesbian Passover ceremony at Camp Sister Spirit in Mississippi. She toured the US with two one-woman plays: *Passing,* on Jewish women's identity and *Revenge of the Women's Studies Professor* — now a successful book — on backlash against feminist scholars. Her essay on Palestine/Israel won first prize in the Nob Hill Penwoman Literary Contest in January 2012.

Ibrahim Muhawi was born in Palestine and received his education in English literature at the University of California, Davis. He taught literature, Arabic folklore, and translation studies at universities in Canada, the Middle East, North Africa, Europe, and the U.S. His publications include *Speak, Bird, Speak Again: Palestinian Arab folktales.* In addition to *Journal of an Ordinary Grief,* he has also translated Mahmoud Darwish's *Memory for Forgetfulness,* and a book of very short stories by the Syrian writer, Zakaria Tamer.

Dana Negev is an Israeli/American writer, teacher and peace activist. She lives in Santa Fe, New Mexico, but travels often to Israel and is involved in the ongoing pursuit of peace. In 2006 her poetry book, *I Om the World,* was released by Earth Medicine Books.

Jerry Newman taught in the Creative Writing Department of the University of British Columbia for many years, has published two novels, *We Always Take Care of Our Own* (McClelland & Stewart, 1964) and *A Russian Novel* (The New Press, 1973), one volume of poems: *Sudden Proclamations* (Cacanada Press, 1998) and one children's picture book: *Green Earrings and a Felt Hat* (Henry Holt, 1993) as well as stories and poems in various literary magazines.

Naomi Shihab Nye is the author and/or editor of more than thirty volumes. Her poetry collections include *Red Suitcase, Words Under the Words, Fuel,* and *You & Yours.* Her novels for young readers include *Habibi, Mint Snowball,* and *Sitti's Secrets.* She published 8 prize winning poetry anthologies for young readers, including *The Space Between Our Footsteps: Poems & Paintings from the Middle East,* and

Honeybee, which won the 2008 Arab American Book Award in the Children's/Young Adult category. Two new books, *There Is No Long Distance Now* (a collection of very short stories) and *Transfer* (poems) appeared in Fall 2011.

Alicia Ostriker teaches in the Low-Residency Poetry MFA Program of Drew University. She has published thirteen poetry collections, including *The Book of Seventy*, which received the 2009 National Jewish Book Award for Poetry. *The Crack in Everything* and *The Little Space: Poems Selected and New, 1969-1989*, were both National Book Award finalists. She is also the author of several books wrestling with the Bible: *Nakedness of the Fathers: Biblical Visions and Revisions* (1994), *The Volcano Sequence* (2002), and *For the Love of God: the Bible as an Open Book* (2007).

Sandy Polishuk is author of *Sticking to the Union: An Oral History of the Life and Times of Julia Ruuttila* (Palgrave Macmillan, 2003), and a producer of the Northwest Women's History Project's "Good Works Sister! Women Shipyard Workers of World War II; an Oral History." Her articles and reviews have appeared in the *Journal of American History*, *Oral History Review*, *Oregon Historical Quarterly*, *Notable American Women*, *Frontiers*, *Travelers' Tales Food*, and *Bridges*, among others. She lives in Portland, Oregon, where she continues working for the reconciliation of the Middle East conflict by serving as co-chair of J Street, Portland.

Nizar Qabbani (1923–1998) was a Syrian diplomat and poet revered by generations of Arabs for his sensual and romantic verse. His work was featured not only in his two dozen volumes of poetry and in regular contributions to the Arabic-language newspaper *Al Hayat*, but in lyrics sung by Lebanese and Syrian vocalists who helped popularize his work. His poetic style combines simplicity and elegance in exploring themes of love, eroticism, feminism, religion, and Arab nationalism. A man of his times and of all times, he is by far the most popular contemporary poet in the Arab world.

Samih al-Qasim, born in 1939, is a Palestinian Druze whose poetry is well-known throughout Arab World. He explains, "While I was still at primary school the Palestinian tragedy occurred. I regard that date as the date of my birth, because the first images I can remember are of the 1948 events." His poetry is influenced by two primary periods of his life: before and **after** the Six-Day War. He joined the Communist Hadash political party in 1967. His several volumes of poetry reflect continuous experimentation with language and tone.

Yousef el Qedra is a young poet and playwright living in Gaza. He has a BA degree in Arabic literature from al Azhar University, Gaza. Since 2006, he has worked as a project coordinator of theatre and youth groups for the Cultural Free Thought Association in Gaza City, Palestine Occupied Territories. He teaches drama, literature and writing. He has written, directed and acted in several plays, and has written four books. Some of his poems have been published in French and Spanish translation.

Diab Rabie (October 10, 1922 - July 14, 2010) was the last in a group of five Diaspora poets which included Kahlil Gibran, Michael Naimeh, and Elie Abu-Madi. A newspaperman assigned to New York, he was prevented by Israelis from reentering his homeland and settled in North Carolina. His poems were published in major Arabic newspapers and magazines around the world throughout his life. His collected poems, entitled *Shetharat El-Rabie* (The Birzeit Society, 2010), were edited by George Khoury and published before his death.

Monica Raymond, a poet, playwright, performer currently based in Cambridge, Massachusetts has taught writing at Harvard, the City University of New York, and the Boston Museum School. She was a 2008-9 Jerome Fellow at the Playwrights' Center. Her play, *The Owl Girl*, won the Clauder Competition Gold Medal, the Peace and Justice Prize, a political theater award, and was featured at Portland Stage's "Little Festival of the Unexpected." Raymond chaired a panel on theater in Israel/Palestine for ATHE (Association for Theater in Higher Education) and performed in *An Olive on the Seder Plate*, a touring revue about Israeli human rights abuses.

Jeremy Reed is writer, poet and prose stylist. He has published fifty works in twenty-five years. He has written more than two dozen books of poetry, twelve novels, and volumes of literary and music criticism. He has also published translations of Montale, Cocteau, Nasrallah, Adonis, Bogary and Hölderlin. His own work has been translated abroad in numerous editions and more than a dozen languages. He has received awards from the National Poetry, Somerset Maugham, Eric Gregory, Ingram Merrill, and Royal Literary Funds. He has also been awarded the Poetry Society's European Translation Prize.

Gavriel Reisner, a teacher, critic, and poet, lectured in English for many years at both Hebrew and Tel Aviv Universities. He is now Lead Teacher for English and AP Literature at the High School of Economics & Finance in New York City. The author of *The Death-*

Ego and the Vital Self: Romances of Desire in Literature and Psychoanalysis (Associated University Press), he also regularly reviews books for *The Psychoanalytic Review*. Reisner was honored to be the companion and husband of Ruth Stein, the psychoanalyst and theorist, for a dozen wonderful years before her recent untimely death.

Marjorie Stamm Rosenfeld is a former U.S. Navy missile analyst, Southern Methodist University Press manuscript editor, and SMU English instructor who has done poetry therapy with forensic patients at St. Elizabeths Hospital, Washington, D.C. Her poetry has been published nationally and internationally in journals and anthologies such as *Southwest Review*, *Nimrod*, *Rosebud* and *Margie*, and on the Internet in *qarrtsiluni*, at MidEastWeb, and in *Zwoje*, where one of her poems appears in Polish translation as well as in English.

Vivien Sansour is a writer, poet and photographer who grew up in Beit Jala, Palestine, received BA and MA degrees from East Carolina University, and is now Media and Promotion Manager for the Canaan Fair Trade Association. She captures stories of Palestinian farmers for the wider world, practicing agriculture as a form of resistance to military occupation. She co-founded *ImaginAction* which, through its Olive Tree Circus, helps farmers access their olive fields during harvest. She has been an activist and organizer in six countries, and now divides her time residing in Los Angeles and Jenin, Palestine.

Willa Schneberg received the Oregon Book Award in Poetry for *In The Margins Of The World*. Willa's Jewish-related poems have appeared in *Tikkun*, *Bridges* and *Drash*. She organizes a yearly reading series of Jewish writers at the Oregon Jewish Museum in Portland. A visual artist, her *The Books of Esther* was displayed at O.J.M. in 2012. In 1987–1988 she volunteered for Sherut La'am, (Service to the People), an Israeli organization comparable to the Peace Corps. She returned to Israel, shortly after the death of Yasser Arafat to judge a poetry competition.

Adam Schonbrun has published eight poetry collections, most recently *New and Selected Poems* (2008). His *An Image of an Angel* won the 1985 Ron Adler Memorial Poetry Prize. His poetry has appeared in the *Jerusalem Post*, *Caesura*, *Puerto del Sol*, and *The Forward*. He has a BA from Haifa University and an MFA in Creative Writing from Penn State University, where he was Katey Lehman Fellow in Poetry. He was Visiting Scholar at the Oxford Center for Hebrew and

Jewish Studies and has taught at Safed College since 1995. He lives in Safed, Galilee with his wife and five children.

Aftab Yusuf Shaikh is an Indian of Arab descent, born and brought up in Mumbai. He writes in English, Hindi, Urdu and Marathi. His work has been featured in *The Istanbul Literary Review*, *Muse India*, *Ancient Heart Magazine*, *Skipping Stones*, and other publications. He has published a collection of poems, *Poems — Twenty Ten* and nine books for children.

Richard E. Sherwin lives in Israel. He is retired from teaching English literature at Bar Ilan University. He loves his family, Israel and Gd, though doesn't profess to understand them; also loves bagpipe music, plainchant, and ballads; and enjoys studying, teaching, and seaside walking and talking.

Scot Siegel lives in Oregon with his wife and two daughters, is an urban planning consultant and serves on the board of the Friends of William Stafford. He published *Some Weather* (Plain View Press, 2008); *Untitled Country* (Pudding House Publications, 2009) and *Skeleton Says* (Finishing Line Press, 2010). His poetry was nominated for a 2009 Pushcart Prize. He has received awards from *Aesthetica Magazine* (UK) and *Nimrod International* (Pablo Neruda Poetry Prize, semi-finalist) and the Oregon State Poetry Association (OSPA). *Poetry Northwest* and the Oregon State Library selected *Some Weather* as one of one-hundred-fifty Outstanding Oregon Poetry Books.

Johnmichael Simon, born in England, grew up in South Africa and has lived in Israel since 1963. A retired technical writer, he has published three solo books of poems and two collaborations with partner Helen Bar-Lev. His poetry and short stories have won prizes in the Ruben Rose Poetry Competition and the Margaret Reid Poetry Contest. He has published widely in print and website collections. He is the chief editor of Cyclamens and Swords Publishing.

Yasmin Snounu, born in Gaza City, Palestine, has a BA degree in English and French from Al Azhar University. As an undergraduate, she volunteered in many non-governmental organizations (NGOs) and later worked for the Women's Affairs Center, an NGO that promotes the welfare of women in Gaza. She lived at home with her family through Israel's Operation Cast Lead attack on Gaza in December 2008 - January 2009. As a Fulbright scholar, she earned an MA in the Teaching of English as a Second Language from Eastern Michigan University. She has co-translated two volumes of Arabic poetry into English.

269

Molly Spencer is a poet, an avid reader of poetry and almost anything else, and a mother of three. Her work has appeared or is forthcoming in *Literary Mama*, *Adanna*, *Calyx* and elsewhere. Her poem, "The Mail Order Bride Attempts a Letter home" has been featured in the online magazine *Linebreak*. A native Michiganian and erstwhile Minnesotan, she now lives in the San Francisco Bay Area with her husband and their children.

Miriam Stanley has performed in the United States and Israel. Her two books of poetry are *Not To Be Believed* (Rogue Scholars Press, 2004) and *Get Over It* (Rogue Scholars Press, 2009). She is also included in the anthologies *Skyscrapers, Taxis, and Tampons* (Fly-by-Night Press, 1999) and *Voices Israel* (2008 and 2009). She was a member of the Fatoosh Ensemble, a multicultural poetry troupe that focuses on the Mideast.

Sabena Stark is a writer and musician. Her poem, "Love After the Holocaust" won Honorable Mention in the Anna Davidson Rosenberg Award for Poetry on the Jewish Experience. She composed the title song of the album "Learning How to Fly," recorded by the jazz duo Tuck and Patti (Epic/Sony). Sabena Stark's book in progress received the 2008 Oregon Literary Arts Fellowship for Literary Nonfiction. She wrote the poem "High Holy Days" while living and writing in Jerusalem. She currently makes her home in Eugene, Oregon.

Hannah Stein was born in Brooklyn, grew up in rural New York, and now lives and writes in Davis, California. Her collection, *Earthlight*, was published by La Questa Press, and her chapbooks include *Schools of Flying Fish* and *Greatest Hits of Hannah Stein, 1981-2004*. Recent and forthcoming poems, and essays on contemporary poetry, appear widely in journals such as *Poetry Flash*, *Nimrod*, *Zeek*, *Chautauqua*, and the *American Literary Review*. She is a member of Jewish Peace Alternatives, a group of concerned citizens in Davis.

Doreen Stock lives in Sausalito, California. During seven years of travel in the '90s, she composed several collections of poems, including *Memorial Service* and *Poems of Arad*, and the essays which eventually became *On Leaving Jerusalem: Prose of a Traveling Nature*.

Erik Sutter-Kaye has been living in Japan since 1998 with his American partner, Corinne. A teacher by trade, an artist by inclination, Erik has had four one-man shows and has been in several group shows in Kamakura and Tokyo.

Richard Tillinghast, an American ex-patriot in Ireland, is the author of ten poetry books, most recently *The New Life*, *Selected Poems* and *Dirty August*, co-translated with Julia Clare Tillinghast-Akalin from the Turkish poet, Edip Cansever. In 2008 he published *Finding Ireland: A Poet's Explorations of Irish Literature and Culture*. He has received grants from the National Endowment for the Arts, the Irish Arts Council, and is a Guggenheim Fellow. Tillinghast has also been awarded the James Dickey Prize for poetry and the Cleanth Brooks Prize for creative nonfiction. He lives in South Tipperary.

Fadwa Tuqan (1917- 2003), born in Nablus, Palestine, was known as the "Poet of Palestine." Her poetry explores love, social protest and patriotism. Tuqan received the International Poetry Award in Palermo, Italy, the Jerusalem Award for Culture and Arts from the PLO and the United Arab Emirates Award. She was awarded the Honorary Palestine Prize for Poetry in 1996 and was the subject of a documentary film directed by novelist Liana Bader in 1999. Tuqan died on December 12, 2003, during the height of the Al-Aqsa Intifada, while her hometown of Nablus was under siege.

J. Weintraub has published fiction, essays, and poetry in such periodicals as *Massachusetts Review*, *The New Criterion*, *Comstock Review*, *Karamu*, *Ascent*, *Bellevue Literary Review*, *The MacGuffin*, *Whetstone*, *Cream City Review*, and in various anthologies. He has been the recipient of writing awards from the Illinois and Barrington Arts Councils, was an *Around the Coyote* poet, and has been a featured reader in the *Twilight Tales* series at Chicago's Red Lion Pub.

Ingrid Wendt's poetry has won the Editions Prize, the Yellowglen Award, and the Oregon Book Award. Her first poetry book, *Moving the House*, was chosen for BOA Editions by William Stafford. Her latest is *Evensong*. She coedited two poetry anthologies, taught at Antioch University and was a three-time Fulbright Professor in Germany. For years she taught K-12 poetry writing; her *Starting With Little Things: A Guide to Writing Poetry in the Classroom* is now in its 6th printing. Ingrid lives in Oregon with husband, poet and writer, Ralph Salisbury. She spent a week in 1995 on the Sinai Peninsula.

Carolyne Wright is the author of nine poetry collections, four volumes of translations, and a collection of essays. Her latest, *Mania Klepto: the Book of Eulene*, was published in 2011. Her *A Change of Maps* won the 2007 IPPY Bronze Award, and *Seasons of Mangoes and Brainfire* won the Blue Lynx Prize and the American Book Award. A year on a Fulbright grant in Chile and four years in India and

Bangladesh engendered award-winning narratives. A visiting writer at colleges and universities, Wright served on the Board of AWP. She lives in Seattle, teaching for the Northwest Institute of Literary Arts' Whidbey Writers Workshop MFA Program.

Tawfiq Zayyad is a Palestinian poet and political writer, educated in Nazareth and Moscow; he has struggled for the rights of Palestinians in Israel through the communist organization, *Rakah.* His poetry collections include *Warmly I Shake Your Hands* (1966), which is regarded as a landmark in the history of the Palestinian struggle against Israel. It includes many poems of courage and resistance, some of which have been adapted to music and have become part of the lively tradition of Palestinian songs of struggle.

PERMISSIONS

Khaled Abdallah: "Slumber," "Mint," "Exchange," and "Empty" were published in *Banipal* (15-16, Autumn 2002/Spring 2003). Reprinted by permission of *Banipal*.

Adonis (Ali Ahmad Said Esber): "Concerto for Jerusalem" (excerpt) translated by Khaled Mattawa, was published in *Banipal 41*. Reprinted by permission of Khaled Mattawa and *Banipal*.

Dr. Ada Aharoni: "This Cursed War" and "Remember Me Every Time" are from her book, *You and I can Change the World* (Lachman, Haifa 1999). Reprinted by permission of the author.

Maryna Ajaja: "Reply" appeared in *The Raven Chronicles*, and appears on the *Poets Against the War* website.

Seema V. Atalla: "Gift" and "Cold Comfort" reprinted from *We Begin Here: Poems for Palestine and Lebanon*, edited by Kamal Boullata and Kathy Engel (Interlink Press, 2007). "Visiting the West Bank" was first published in *Mediterraneans*, 1994. Reprinted by permission of the author.

Ellen Bass: "Moonlight" appeared in *Zeek* magazine (Winter 2009).

Elana Bell: "On a hilltop at the Nassar Farm in the West Bank Overlooking the Surrounding Settlement of Neve Daniel" first appeared in *CALYX Journal* in June 2011.

Tom Berman: "greening days, " appeared in *Poeticdiversity* e-zine in December 2007.

Gloria Bletter: "No Safe Sky" appeared in the *National Lawyers Guild Newsletter* (Spring 2010).

Judith Brice: A version of "Questions of Betrayal" appeared in the *Paterson Literary Review*, and has been made a part of the permanent archives of the Holocaust Memorial Center in Farmington Hills, Michigan.

Rachel Barenblat: "In the Same Key" was originally published in *70 Faces, Torah Poems* (Phoenicia Publishing, 2011).

Reja-e Busailah: "In the Shadow of the Holy Heights" is reprinted from *We Begin Here: Poems for Palestine and Lebanon*, edited by Kamal Boullata and Kathy Engel (Interlink Press, 2007). Reprinted by permission of Reja-e Busailah and Interlink Books.

Rachel Corrie: *E-mail to her Mother, February 27, 2003* is from *Let Me Stand Alone, The Journals of Rachel Corrie* by Rachel Corrie, edited by the Corrie Family. Copyright © 2008 by Craig and Cindy Corrie. Used by permission of Craig and Cindy Corrie and W.W. Norton & Company, Inc..

Mahmoud Darwish: Excerpts from his *Journal of an Ordinary Grief*, translated by Ibrahim Muhawi, reprinted by permission of Ibrahim Muhawi and Archipelago Books. "Concerning Hopes," reprinted from *The Palestinian Wedding: A Bilingual Anthology of Contemporary Palestinian Resistance Poetry*, collected and translated by A. M. Elmessiri (Three Continents Press, 1982). Used by permission of Lynne Rienner Publishing, Inc.

Sharon Doubiago: performed "Playing Oslo Pool with Mahmoud Darwish" at the October 5, 2008 Bird & Beckett **A Day for Mahmoud Darwish** reading in San Francisco.

Merle Feld: "Bikur Cholim," appeared in *A Spiritual Life* (SUNY Press, 2007). Reprinted by permission of SUNY Press.

Ruth Fogelman: "Jerusalem, City of Prayer" appears in her recent volume of poetry, *Cradled in God's Arms,* published by Alon Sefer (Israel, 2009). Reprinted by permission of the author.

CB Follett: "Palestine," was previously published in *Question Everything, Challenge Everything,* 1997.

David Gershator: "Dividing Jerusalem" appeared in *Home Planet News* (Issue 47, Spring 2001). "Bad Weather Blessing" appeared in *Home Planet News* (Issue 49, Spring 2003).

Reuven Goldfarb: "Sitting Down at My Computer on Motzaei Shabbat" appeared in *Poetica Magazine* (July 2005).

Marian Haddad: "The Map on My Friend's Wall" first appeared under another title in *Scheherazade's Legacy,* edited by Susan Muaddi Darraj (Praeger, 2004), reprinted by permission of Marian Haddad and Susan Muaddi Darraj

Sam Hamod: "There Must Be Something Dangerous About a Zoo in Rafah, Palestine" and a version of "Sabra/Shatilla: In Sorrow" appeared in *We Begin Here: Poems for Palestine and Lebanon*, edited by Kamal Boullata and Kathy Engel (Interlink Publishing Group, 2007). Reprinted by permission of Sam Hamod and Interlink Press.

Hadassah Haskale: "Grapes of Peace/ Inaab Salaam" was first published in *Palestine-Israel Journal of Politics, Economics and Culture* (Volume 11, Numbers 3 & 4, 2004/5) and subsequently in her book *Dreaming Beyond War* (Mazo Publishers, Jerusalem, 2005).

Sam Hazo: "Intifada," appears in *We Begin Here: Poems for Palestine and Lebanon*, edited by Kamal Boullata and Kathy Engel, reprinted by permission of Interlink Press and Sam Hazo. "For Fawzi in Jerusalem" appears in *Blood Rights* (University of Pittsburgh Press, 1968). "Mediterranean Update" and "Suffer the Little Children," appear in *The Song of the Horse* (Autumn House Press, 2008).

Lahab Assef al-Jundi: "Holy Landers" appeared in the *Texas Observer,* (September 7, 2007), and in Sam Hamod's *Today's Alternative News* on April 29, 2010. "Holy Landers" and "Collateral Savage" were featured in *In These Latitudes: Ten Contemporary Poets,* published by Wings Press in 2008.

Sami Al Jundi: "Take Me to Al-Qastal" appears in *The Hour of Sunlight* (Nation Books, 2011), reprinted by permission of Nation Books.

Judy Kronenfeld: "Clean" appeared on the website, *New Verse News* (May 23, 2007). "This War" was first published in *Calyx* (Volume 24, Number 3, Summer, 2008).

Joy Ladin: "A Strand of Thick Black Hair" and "The Situation: An Exclusive Simulcast" published in *Alternatives to History* (Sheep Meadow Press, 2003). "Heaven's Gate" appeared in *Ha-Aretz Magazine* (May 16, 2002) and in the *New York Times* (January 6, 2003).

Mike Maggio: "Oranges from Palestine," "Dirge," and "Sunday Morning—Amman" appeared in *Oranges from Palestine* (Mardi Gras Press, 1996). Reprinted by permission of the author. "Dirge" also appeared in *Live Poets* (Issue 1, 1991), in excerpt form in Vol. No. Magazine, #19, Fall,1992, and in *Identity Theory* (www.identitytheory.com) July 2003.

Susan Martin: "Global Warming " appeared in *Exit 13* (Issue 15, 2008).

Philip Metres: 3 poems from *Along the Shrapnel Edge of Maps* by permission of the author.

David Miller: "Memories of the Wailing Wall" originally appeared in a slightly different form in *Half Drunk Muse* (Winter 2005).

Bonnie J. Morris, Ph.D.: "A Poetry Slam with God" was read in Washington, D.C. at the women's spoken-word stage, *Mothertongue,* where Dr. Morris often emcees.

Naomi Shihab Nye: "How Palestinians Keep Warm," "Jerusalem" and "Shoulders" are from *Red Suitcase.* "Knowing" and "Hello Palestine," appear in *Transfer* (BOA Editions, 2011). All 5 poems reprinted by permission of BOA Editions.

Alicia Ostriker: "What Is Needed After Food" from *No Heaven* (University of Pittsburgh Press, 2005). Reprinted by permission of University of Pittsburgh Press.

Sandy Polishuk: "Possession" first appeared in *PS: The Intelligent Guide for Jewish Affairs* #77 (January 22, 1997), and reprinted in the *LA Voice* (February 8, 1997).

Nizar Qabanni: "An Invitation for the Fifth of June" and "Jerusalem," were reprinted from *On Entering the Sea: The Erotic and Other Poetry of Nizar Qabbani*, edited by Salma Khadra Jayyusi (1996). Reprinted by permission of Interlink Books.

Yousef el Qedra: "Exhaustion Overtook Me," "On the Margin of a Whirlwind," and "I Have No Home" were translated from the Arabic by Edward Morin and Yasmin Snounu, and appeared in *The Dirty Goat* (Number 24, February 2011).

Samih al-Qasim: Excerpt from "After the Apocalypse" from *Modern Arabic Poetry,* edited by Salma Khadra Jayyusi. (Columbia University Press, 1991) Reprinted with permission of the publisher. "A Homeland" and "Letter from a Prison Camp" are reprinted from *The Palestinian Wedding: A Bilingual Anthology of Contemporary Palestinian Resistance Poetry*, collected and translated by A. M. Elmessiri (Three Continents Press, 1982). Used by permission of Lynne Rienner Publishing, Inc.

Diab Rabie: "Swearing by Your Jerusalem," translated by George Khoury and Edward Morin, was first published in the Arabic language newspaper, *Sameer*, in New York City in 1947, and in *Shetharat El-Rabie (The Poems of El-Rabie)*, edited by George Khoury (Birzeit Society, 2010). Reprinted by permission of George Khoury and the Birzeit Society.

Monica Raymond: "In Cana" appeared in the *Colorado Review* in 2007 and online at *versedaily.org*.

Gavriel Reisner: "Two Stories," in a slightly different version, has been accepted for publication in *Arc-21*.

Marjorie Stamm Rosenfeld: *"Tzama"* and "Here-There Spring" appear online at *MidEastWeb* (www.mideastweb.org/poetry.htm).

Willa Schneberg: An earlier and somewhat different version of "An Attempt at Hastening the Messianic Age" appeared in the *Cincinnati Judaica Review* (Volume III, Spring 1992).

Adam Schonbrun: "Chana of the Ages" appeared in *Puerto Del Sol* (1991). "Messianic Hot Pepper Poem" appeared in *The Jewish Quarterly* (1996).

Richard E. Sherwin: A version of "my friends & i" appeared online in the *Menorah Review*.

Scot Siegel: "Lucky Star" first appeared in *Drash: Northwest Mosaic* (Volume III, 2009). It also appears in his chapbook, *Untitled Country* (Pudding House Publications, 2009). Reprinted by permission of the author.

Johnmichael Simon: "Morning at the Shuk" and "Waters of Gaza" appeared in *Cyclamens and Swords* (Ibbetson Street Press, 2007).

Hannah Stein: "Body Parts," appeared in *The Sow's Ear* (August 2008).

Doreen Stock: "Girl's Burial/Gaza 2009" appeared in *Seal Report* (January 2010).

Yasmin Snounu: "Inside the Flame of the Cast Lead," under the title of "Massacre in Cast Lead" was published online at *Virtual Gaza* on January 18, 2009.

Richard Tillinghast: "What is Not Allowed" has appeared online and in the *Irish Times* (June 5, 2010). Audio versions have appeared on *YouTube*.

Fadwa Tuqan: "I Shall Not Weep," translated by Naomi Shihab Nye and Salma Khadra Jayussi, appeared in Tuqan's autobiography, *A Mountainous Journey*, translated into English by Olive Kenny, edited by Khadra Jayyusi (Graywolf Press, 1990). Reprinted by permission of Naomi Shihab Nye. "My Sad City" is reprinted from *The Palestinian Wedding: A Bilingual Anthology of Contemporary Palestinian Resistance Poetry*, collected and translated by A. M. Elmessiri (Three Continents Press, 1982). Used by permission of Lynne Rienner Publishing, Inc.

J. Weintraub: "To the Diamond Peddler, Steinberg/Postmark: Beirut/No Return Address/1979"first appeared in *Hyperion,* (Volume III, Number 6, 1980).

Ingrid Wendt: "Surgeonfish," reprinted from *Surgeonfish* (WordTech Editions, 2005).

Carolyne Wright: "Round: Before the Start of the Long War" was previously published in *The Iowa Review* (Volume 38, Number 2, 2008).

Tawfiq Zayyad: "Before Their Tanks," "Here We Will Stay," "Passing Remark," "Salman," and "They Know," translated by Sharif Elmusa and Charles Doria, appeared in *Modern Arabic Poetry: An Anthology* (Columbia University Press, 1987). Reprinted by permission of Columbia University Press.